The Best of Casual Mexican Cooking

CANTINA

Published in Great Britain in 1997 by
Prion Books Ltd.,
32-34 Gordon House Road,
London NW5 1LP

Produced by
WELDON OWEN INC.
President: John Owen
Vice President and Publisher: Wendely Harvey
Vice President and CFO: Richard VanOosterhout
Managing Editor: Lisa Chaney Atwood
Consulting Editor and Introductory Text: Norman Kolpas
Copy Editor: Sharon Silva
Design: Patty Hill
Production Director: Stephanie Sherman
Production Coordinator: Tarji Mickelson
Production Editor: Janique Gascoigne
Editorial Assistant: Sarah Lemas
Co-Editions Director: Derek Barton
Foreign Editions Production Manager: Jen Dalton
Food Photography: Joyce Oudkerk Pool
Food Stylist: Stephanie Greenleigh
Prop Stylist: Carol Hacker
Assistant Food Stylist: Claudia Breault
Half-Title Illustration: Martha Anne Booth
Chapter Opener Illustrations: Faranak
Glossary Illustrations: Alice Harth

Produced in Singapore by Kyodo Printing Co.

ISBN 1-85375-245-2

A Note on Weights and Measures:
All recipes include customary U.S. and metric measurements.
Metric conversions are based on a standard developed for these
books and have been rounded off. Actual weights may vary.

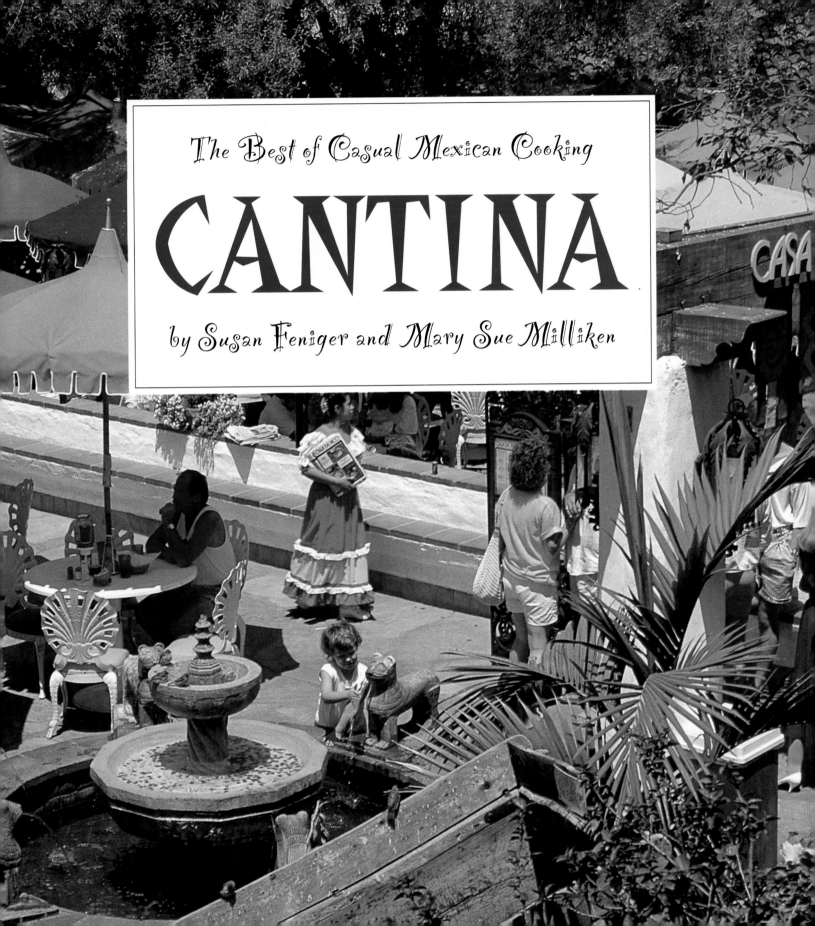

The Best of Casual Mexican Cooking

CANTINA

by Susan Feniger and Mary Sue Milliken

Contents

Introduction 7

Appetizers 17

Salads 37

Soups and Stews 53

Main Courses 81

Desserts 103

Introduction

*T*he scene repeats itself in every Mexican village and city. Along town squares and scattered in public markets, little family-owned stalls—often merely a table, a portable stove and two or three chairs—serve homemade regional specialties.

Humble as such trappings might be, however, there is nothing humble about the food: *chile verde,* a stew of pork and green chilies; *albóndigas,* a fragrant meatball soup; *tacos de carne asada,* grilled steak enfolded in corn tortillas. Workers stop by for a quick bite. Young courting couples, with an aunt in tow, enjoy the chaperoned intimacy of a shared snack. Mothers bolster their children's flagging energy with a quesadilla or a frothy *licuado.*

Such casual dining extends to larger establishments as well: bars where guacamole and tortilla chips accompany the beer; white-tiled delicatessens with platters of chiles rellenos; or rustic restaurants that welcome three generations for a Sunday meal.

Whatever the venue, a similar spirit reigns. That spirit is best summoned, perhaps, by the word *cantina,* which suggests the air of relaxation, friendship, value and good food common to them all.

Cantina History

While all cuisines are hybrids, developing under diverse cultural, social and historical influences, the roots of Mexican cooking may be traced more easily than most. For centuries, the native populations of the country ate stews and roasts featuring such indigenous ingredients as turkey, quail and seafood, along with three staples that later found their way to the Old World—squashes, beans and corn—and two lively seasonings that provided distinctive personality: chocolate and chilies.

Spanish explorers and settlers, starting with the arrival of Hernán Cortés and his men at the Aztec court in 1519, brought with them a whole new bill of fare that would influence Mexican cooking. Onions, garlic, citrus fruits, sugarcane, wheat, rice, chicken, beef and, most notably, pork, entered the nation's kitchens. Not only did pork become a featured ingredient of the cuisine, but abundant lard introduced an important new cooking method, frying. As noted Anglo-Mexican cooking authority Elisabeth Lambert Ortiz once observed, "It would be an exaggeration to say that modern Mexican cooking is Aztec cooking plus pigs, but the statement is not far out of line."

This edible intermingling of cultures took place throughout the land, and perhaps most dynamically in Spanish convents and missions, which, by offering bed and board to travelers, also became early restaurants of a sort. Mexico's national dish, *mole poblano de guajalote,* was even developed, so the story goes, as a piece of divinely inspired culinary serendipity by 16th-century nuns scurrying to put together a dinner worthy of a visiting archbishop. They cooked wild turkey in a smooth, rich sauce that combined indigenous chilies, tomatoes, cornmeal and chocolate with such newcomers as onions, garlic, almonds and grapes to make a whole far greater than the sum of its many parts.

Such serendipity is a signature of cantina-style food to this day. In market stalls and neighborhood restaurants

CANTINA: THE BEST OF CASUAL MEXICAN COOKING

alike, proprietors will take the best the season has to offer, combine it with the best of their family's heritage and their personal cooking skills and inspirations and offer up humble tastes of Mexico's culinary history.

The Cantina Experience

Whether they're called bars, *cafeterías*, *restaurantes* or, yes, cantinas, the casual restaurants of Mexico offer the food of the common working folk. Far from the tourist traps of the main thoroughfares, they are more likely to be found tucked into residential neighborhoods, on out-of-the-way plazas or in the marketplaces where the locals shop.

Menus reflect the nation's diverse regional specialties: grilled or dried beef in the north; exotic Mayan-style tamales wrapped in banana leaves in the Yucatán; lobster tacos at a palm-thatched beachside hut in Acapulco; or chicken simmered in one of the seven legendary mole sauces of Oaxaca.

A bar or a market stall will probably provide just one such specialty, the simpler to prepare and eat the better. As the establishment grows grander—in size, but certainly not in pretensions—it might present a menu of half a dozen or so dishes, listed in writing as well as portrayed in a brightly colored mural emblazoned on a once-vacant wall. On a larger scale still, a wide array of foods might be displayed in large earthenware dishes on a buffet line, ready for guests to point at and order.

Today, the casual cantina approach to dining finds its way north of the border, too, where many American restaurants—especially in the southwestern and western states—serve their own traditional and contemporary interpretations of Mexican, New Mexican, Tex-Mex and Cal-Mex food. The trappings may be trendier, with colorful wall decorations and piped-in mariachi music, and the restaurant may, more likely than not, even include the word *cantina* in its name. But, from the first sip of a margarita with guacamole and chips, through a Mexican-inspired main course with its mandatory rice and beans, to the final soothing spoonful of flan, every aspect of the meal will aim to make you feel part of a large, warmhearted gathering. And, in that respect, even the trendiest cantina experience brings you back in touch with the most basic snack eaten at a bustling south-of-the-border market stall.

Bringing the Cantina Home

Perhaps the simplest, most vivid way to transform your own kitchen or dining room into a cantina is to bring the Mexican marketplace home. Bowls heaped full of red and green chili peppers or sun-toned tropical fruits brighten any room, no matter what its other trappings might be.

Let the foods you cook from this book decorate your table as well. Arrange them in large, rustic earthenware casseroles or bowls and serve them family style. Select sturdy, colorful Mexican or other tableware that captures the same spirit.

Add to the table other touches that contribute lively colors and patterns. Use a bright woven fabric as a tablecloth, for example. Or set out vases of bold flowers, whether real ones gathered from your yard or oversized paper creations picked up at a local crafts shop.

Beverages

Cantina cuisine is so widely varied in its ingredients and seasonings that you can pair it with just about any beverage you choose. Mexicans themselves have available a diversity of selections, each of which seems well suited to a particular type of food, time of day or occasion, yet versatile enough to be served with nearly any dish.

Aguas Frescas and Licuados

Simplest of all are beverages based largely on fresh fruit. *Aguas frescas,* literally "fresh waters," may be found throughout Mexico, on street-stall and restaurant counters alike. Simple mixtures of fresh, pulpy fruit juice, mineral water and sugar, they slake the thirst on a hot afternoon, while perfectly complementing a taco or other snack. Prominently displayed, they are ladled from large glass jars filled with chunks of ice and displayed side by side, the better to contrast the vibrant, natural colors of such flavors as watermelon, mango, lime, orange, pineapple and such local favorites as tamarindo, made from the tart-sweet pulp of the tamarind tree, and Jamaica, a tea brewed from spicy-sweet hibiscus blossoms. Also worthy of mention is *horchata,* a soothing *agua* usually based on ground white rice, sometimes with the addition of almonds, and flavored with cinnamon.

Fresh fruit finds its way as well into *licuados,* Mexico's answer to smoothies. Mixed in an electric blender, these combine chunks of fruit with ice and milk to make frothy drinks that, like their American cousins, often serve as a breakfast substitute or afternoon pick-me-up for people on the go.

Beer

When somewhat more fortifying refreshment is desired, well-chilled beer accompanies cantina food most agreeably, its rich, robust flavor and edge of bitterness complementing the cuisine's earthiness and spice. Mexico's brewing industry, fostered under the brief three-year reign of the Viennese prince Maximilian starting in 1864, is centered in the northern city of Monterrey. But dozens of different beers are now produced across the land, and they may be found with increasing frequency outside the country. Try to find the half bottles—perfect little thirst quenchers—produced by some manufacturers.

Wine

Matching wine with the bold flavors of cantina food presents more of a challenge. As a general rule, fruity wines with just an edge of spice or sweetness stand up well. Among whites, you might want to try those made from Sauvignon Blanc or Semillon grapes; good choices in reds include Cabernet Franc and Zinfandel. Following the age-old wisdom of matching local wines to local foods, you might want to seek

out some of the good vintages being produced in the northern Mexican states of Querétaro, Aguascalientes and Baja California Norte; or venture farther afield to try wines from Argentina, Chile or Spain.

If you aren't feeling quite so adventurous or serious-minded about wine-and-food pairings, there's always sangría. Spain's wine-based fruit punch feels very much at home in Mexican cantinas, ready to quench the thirst and elevate the spirits with a single sip.

Tequila

No cantina beverage, of course, possesses more power to send one's spirit soaring than tequila. Fermented and then distilled from the juicy heart of the blue agave plant, and produced under government law only in the states of Jalisco, Nayarit and Michoacán, this potent liquor is traditionally knocked back neat, with a suck of lime and a lick of salt, or perhaps with a chaser of *sangrita,* a mixture of orange juice, red chilies, lime and salt that jolts away the haze.

For many people, tequila is just a step on the pathway toward the ultimate cantina cocktail, the margarita (see sidebar). But that admittedly wonderful concoction dates from an era when not all tequilas were produced with as much care as they are now. Today's products—whether the silver or gold varieties or, even more so, the *añejo* (aged) tequilas—also reward more thoughtful sipping, much like a fine brandy or Cognac.

Coffee and Chocolate

Coffee production came to Mexico in the late 18th century. Today, it ranks as the country's top export crop, and Mexico stands third among the world's producers of arabica beans. If you like, try brewing freshly ground beans the old-fashioned cantina way, as *café de olla,* or "jug coffee." In an earthenware jug, combine the coarsely ground beans with hot water, raw sugar, cinnamon sticks, strips of orange zest and whole cloves. Let them steep for several minutes, then pour through a fine strainer into heated mugs.

Or for a morning or after-dinner experience that reaches back to ancient times, visit local Mexican markets or specialty-food stores in search of circular tablets of cinnamon-flavored Mexican chocolate, ready to be beaten with hot milk into a frothy drink worthy of an Aztec king.

BORDER MARGARITA

Margaritas are a popular cantina menu offering. Serve blended or shaken and poured over ice.

1 lime slice
  Margarita or kosher salt
2 fl oz (60 ml) *añejo* tequila
1 fl oz (30 ml) orange liqueur such as Grand Marnier
1 fl oz (30 ml) fresh lime juice
  Ice cubes

◧ Gently dampen the rim of a margarita glass with the lime slice. Dip the rim in a saucer of salt to coat.

◧ In a blender or cocktail shaker, combine the tequila, orange liqueur, lime juice and a handful of ice cubes. Blend until smooth, or shake until chilled. Pour the margarita into the prepared glass, adding fresh ice if the margarita was shaken. Slip the lime slice on the rim of the glass and serve.

Serves 1

Basic Recipes

Four basic foods serve as the cornerstones of virtually any cantina meal. Tortillas made from cornmeal or wheat flour are the bread of Mexico. Chili-laced salsas season almost every savory dish, whether during cooking or at the dining table. Beans and rice are such staples that, accompanied with tortillas and salsa, they can form a humble but nutritious meal on their own.

FLOUR TORTILLAS

TORTILLAS DE HARINA

Only slightly more difficult to make than corn tortillas, because of the increased elasticity of the dough, these thin wheat-flour disks of northern Mexico are wonderful served with grilled meats. If you like, you can shape them a day or two in advance and store them in the refrigerator, to be cooked just before serving.

2½   cups (12½ oz/390 g) all-purpose (plain) flour
⅓   cup (3 oz/90 g) plus 2 tablespoons vegetable shortening
1   teaspoon salt
1   cup (8 fl oz/250 ml) warm water

☒ In a bowl, combine the flour, shortening and salt. Using your fingers, rub the ingredients together until completely combined and the mixture looks crumbly. Mix in the warm water until the ingredients come together in a ball. Knead the dough in the bowl until smooth, about 3 minutes.

☒ Divide the dough into 12 equal pieces and roll each piece into a ball. Place the balls on a plate and cover with a kitchen towel or plastic wrap. Let rest in the refrigerator for at least 30 minutes or as long as overnight.

☒ On a lightly floured board, roll out each ball into a thin 6-inch (15-cm) round, frequently turning the rounds over to prevent sticking. Lay the rounds in a single layer on the lightly floured board, cover with kitchen towels and let rest for 30 minutes. Or stack between pieces of parchment (baking) paper or waxed paper, wrap well in plastic wrap and refrigerate for up to 2 days.

☒ To cook, heat a dry griddle or heavy nonstick frying pan over medium heat. One at a time, cook the tortillas, turning once, until puffy and slightly golden, 30–45 seconds on each side. Transfer to a platter lined with a kitchen towel and let cool briefly, then stack and wrap in a damp towel to keep warm.

☒ When all the tortillas are cooked, serve immediately. Or let cool, wrap in plastic wrap and store in the refrigerator for up to 5 days. To reheat, wrap the tortillas in aluminum foil and place in a preheated 350°F (180°C) oven for about 15 minutes.

Makes twelve 6-inch (15-cm) tortillas

CANTINA: THE BEST OF CASUAL MEXICAN COOKING

CORN TORTILLAS

TORTILLAS DE MAIZ

The basic bread of Mexico, freshly made corn tortillas have a rich, earthy aroma and a wonderful flavor to which store-bought varieties simply can't compare. Masa harina, a Mexican-style cornmeal, provides authentic flavor and texture. A comal, an old-fashioned Mexican stove-top griddle, is the ideal cooking surface, although any griddle or pan will do just fine.

2 cups (10 oz/315 g) *masa harina*
  Pinch of salt
1 cup (8 fl oz/250 ml) lukewarm water, or as needed

◙ In a large bowl, combine the *masa harina* and salt. Gradually stir in the 1 cup (8 fl oz/250 ml) lukewarm water until smooth. The dough should be slightly sticky and form a ball when pressed together. To test, flatten a small ball of dough between your palms or 2 sheets of plastic wrap. If the edges crack, add more lukewarm water, a little at a time, until the edges are smooth.

◙ Divide the dough into 12 or 18 pieces, depending upon the size tortillas you need. Roll each piece into a ball. Place the balls on a plate and cover with a damp kitchen towel. Heat a dry griddle, cast-iron frying pan, heavy nonstick pan or *comal* (see note above) over medium heat.

◙ *To form tortillas with a tortilla press*, slit open a heavy-duty plastic bag and use the plastic to line the lower surface of an opened tortilla press, allowing it to extend slightly beyond the edges. Place a ball of dough in the center of the press, top with a second piece of plastic and close the press to flatten the dough. Open the press and carefully peel off the plastic.

◙ *To form tortillas with a rolling pin*, flatten the ball of dough between 2 sheets of plastic wrap on a work surface and roll out to a thickness of about 1/16 inch (2 mm).

◙ Lay the tortillas, one at a time, on the preheated griddle or pan and cook, pressing the top gently with your fingertips to make it puff and turning once, until it appears cooked but not browned, 30–45 seconds on each side.

◙ As the tortillas are cooked, transfer them to a kitchen towel and let cool briefly, then stack and wrap in the towel to keep moist and warm.

◙ When all the tortillas are cooked, serve immediately. Or let cool, wrap in plastic wrap and store in the refrigerator for up to 1 week. To reheat for serving, sprinkle each tortilla with a few drops of water and heat on a preheated nonstick pan for 10–15 seconds on each side. Stack on a kitchen towel and wrap to keep warm until serving.

Makes twelve 6-inch (15-cm) tortillas or eighteen 4-inch (10-cm) tortillas

ÁRBOL SALSA

SALSA DE CHILE DE ÁRBOL

This salsa pairs the rich complexity of roasted tomatoes and tomatillos with peppery árbol chilies. Serve with any dish in need of spice.

1 lb (500 g) plum (Roma) tomatoes, cored
½ lb (250 g) tomatillos, husked
½ cup (1 oz/30 g) dried árbol chili peppers, seeded
1 bunch fresh cilantro (fresh coriander), stemmed
½ small yellow onion, sliced
3 cloves garlic, sliced
1 cup (8 fl oz/250 ml) water
2 teaspoons salt

◙ Preheat a broiler (griller). Place the tomatoes and tomatillos in a shallow baking pan. Broil (grill), turning occasionally, until charred on all sides, 10–12 minutes.

◙ In a small, dry frying pan over medium heat, toast the chilies, turning once, until the skins begin to blister, 3–5 minutes. Transfer the chilies to a saucepan and add the tomatoes, cilantro, onion, garlic, water and salt. Bring to a boil, reduce the heat to medium and simmer until the chilies are soft, 10–12 minutes.

◙ Let cool, then transfer to a blender. Purée until smooth, then strain through a sieve placed over a bowl. Serve warm or at room temperature. To store, cover and refrigerate for up to 5 days or freeze for up to 1 month.

Makes about 2½ cups (20 fl oz/625 ml)

RED SALSA

SALSA ROJA

This all-purpose cooked salsa forms a simple dip for chips, a topping for tacos or enchiladas, a pool of sauce for chiles rellenos or a key flavoring in soups, rices and stews. Variations couldn't be easier: substitute smoky chipotle chilies for the jalapeños, for example, or add chopped cilantro just before serving to give it a fresher flavor.

2 tablespoons vegetable oil
1 yellow onion, thinly sliced
2 cloves garlic, sliced
1 fresh jalapeño chili pepper, stemmed, seeded and thinly sliced
1 teaspoon salt, or to taste
2 cups (12 oz/375 g) canned plum (Roma) tomatoes with their juices

In a saucepan over medium heat, warm the vegetable oil. Add the onion and sauté until soft, about 10 minutes. Add the garlic, chili pepper and salt and cook for 2 minutes longer. Add the tomatoes and their juices and reduce the heat to low. Cook the tomatoes, stirring occasionally to break them up, until soft and the juices have reduced by half, 10–15 minutes.

Let cool slightly, then transfer to a blender. Purée until smooth, then strain through a sieve placed over a bowl. Set aside to cool completely for use as a table salsa. Or reheat gently over low heat to use hot. To store, cover tightly and keep in the refrigerator for up to 4 days or in the freezer for up to 1 month.

Makes about 2 cups (16 fl oz/500 ml)

GREEN SALSA

SALSA VERDE

Bottled green salsa can't compare to freshly made. Whether you use it as a dip, on empanadas or tacos, or cooked in soups or stews, its piquant character perfectly perks up rich flavors.

¾ lb (375 g) tomatillos, husked and quartered
2 fresh serrano chili peppers, coarsely chopped
¼ small yellow onion, sliced
⅓ cup (3 fl oz/80 ml) water
1 teaspoon salt, or as needed
⅓ cup (⅓ oz/10 g) coarsely chopped fresh cilantro (fresh coriander)

In a blender or food processor fitted with the metal blade, combine the tomatillos, chilies, onion and water; process briefly until chunky. Add the 1 teaspoon salt and the cilantro and purée until no large chunks remain, about 2 minutes longer.

Taste and add more salt, if needed. Pour into a bowl and serve, or cover and refrigerate for up to 3 days.

Makes about 2 cups (16 fl oz/500 ml)

REFRIED BEANS

FRIJOLES REFRITOS

No Mexican meal is complete without this creamy staple. Although pinto beans fried in lard are the more traditional choice, black beans fried in vegetable oil meet the more health-conscious demands of today. The beans go best with rice.

2 cups (14 oz/440 g) dried black or pinto beans
8 cups (64 fl oz/2 l) water
⅔ cup (5 oz/155 g) lard or (5 fl oz/160 ml) vegetable oil
1 large yellow onion, diced
1–2 teaspoons salt
½ teaspoon freshly ground pepper Fresh cilantro (fresh coriander) leaves, optional

Sort through the beans and discard any misshapen beans or stones. Rinse well. Place the beans in a saucepan and add the water. Bring to a boil, reduce the heat to medium-low, cover and simmer until the smallest beans are cooked through and creamy inside, about 1½ hours.

Remove the beans from the heat. Using a potato masher, mash the beans with their cooking liquid until evenly mashed.

In a sauté pan over medium heat, warm the lard or oil. Add all but about ¼ cup (1¼ oz/38 g) of the diced onion, salt to taste and pepper and sauté briskly until the onion is translucent and just begins to brown, about 10 minutes. Add the mashed beans and cook, stirring, until the excess liquid evaporates and the beans begin to pull away from the pan sides, about 10 minutes. Cook without stirring until a thin layer of the mashed beans begins to stick to the pan bottom. Scrape up the layer and reincorporate it into the beans. Repeat this step 2 or 3 times, allowing the beans to begin to stick and then scraping them up, until the beans are thick and creamy.

☒ To serve, spoon the beans onto a warmed platter or individual plates and top with the reserved diced onion. Garnish with cilantro, if desired, and serve hot. Store leftover beans, covered, in the refrigerator for up to 4 days. To reheat, return the beans to a wide sauté pan, add a little water and place over medium heat, stirring constantly to heat evenly.

Makes 3–4 cups (24–32 fl oz/ 750 ml–1 l); serves 4–6

STEAMED RICE

ARROZ BLANCO AL VAPOR

Rice was first carried to Mexico on the 16th-century Spanish trade galleons that plied the waters between Manila and Acapulco. It has been an integral part of the diet ever since, often paired with the country's ubiquitous beans.

2   cups (14 oz/440 g) long-grain white rice
3   cups (24 fl oz/750 ml) water
2   tablespoons unsalted butter
1   teaspoon salt

☒ Place the rice in a large bowl (not a colander) and rinse under cold running water for 5 minutes. Drain.

☒ In a saucepan, bring the water to a boil. Add the butter, rice and salt and return to a boil. Reduce the heat to low, cover and cook until the water is absorbed, about 20 minutes.

☒ Remove from the heat and let stand, covered, for a few minutes. Fluff with a fork and serve.

Makes about 5 cups (25 oz/780 g); serves 4–6

RED OR GREEN RICE

ARROZ ROJO O VERDE

These two rice dishes make colorful, tasty accompaniments to simple grilled meats and fish.

2   cups (14 oz/440 g) long-grain white rice
¼   cup (2 fl oz/60 ml) vegetable oil
1   yellow onion, diced
2   cloves garlic, minced
1½   cups (12 fl oz/375 ml) chicken stock
1½   cups (12 fl oz/375 ml) red salsa plus 2 or 3 fresh whole red serrano chili peppers, for red rice
1   cup (8 fl oz/250 ml) green salsa puréed with 3 fresh poblano chili peppers, roasted and peeled *(see glossary, page 125),* for green rice

☒ Place the rice in a large bowl (not a colander) and rinse under cold running water for 5 minutes. Drain.

☒ In a saucepan over high heat, warm the oil. Add the onion and garlic and sauté until golden, about 5 minutes. Add the rice and sauté for 5 minutes longer. Pour in the chicken stock.

☒ For red rice, add the red salsa and serrano chilies; for green rice, add the green salsa and poblano chilies. Bring to a boil. Reduce the heat to low, cover and cook until the stock is absorbed, about 20 minutes.

☒ Remove from the heat and let stand, covered, for a few minutes. Fluff with a fork and serve.

Makes about 5 cups (25 oz/780 g); serves 4–6

INTRODUCTION

Appetizers

exicans might well use the word *antojitos* —"little whimsies"— to describe the recipes on the following pages. The term applies to virtually any dish easily popped into the mouth, whether at the start of a meal or as a snack while strolling through a marketplace.

Like any good starter, these recipes boast impressive versatility. Guacamole, for example, may be scooped up with tortilla chips to accompany beer or sangría; but it also provides a cool, rich garnish for spicy main courses. Ceviche makes an elegant appetizer when presented in a sparkling glass bowl; but you might also see it in a paper cup held in the hand of someone wandering along the seafront in Acapulco or Puerto Vallarta. And empanadas are just as satisfying eaten as a simple lunch as they are a first course.

With that spirit of versatility in mind, you might present a meal composed just of these recipes, perhaps joined by one or two other finger foods, such as beef tacos, grilled beef or chicken drumsticks, that comfortably fit beneath the *antojitos* umbrella. Set them out together on a buffet table, letting guests pick and choose as whimsy dictates.

Roasted Peppers with Melted Cheese

A classic northern Mexican dish, queso fundido—*literally, "melted cheese"—makes a delightful starter for a cold-weather meal. Serve with lots of warm tortillas to scoop up the bubbling mixture. For more spice, add crunchy browned chunks of chorizo sausage or drizzle with árbol salsa (recipe on page 13).*

1 fresh poblano chili pepper, roasted, peeled and seeded *(see glossary, page 125)*

1 red bell pepper (capsicum), roasted, peeled and seeded *(see glossary, page 124)*

1 yellow bell pepper (capsicum), roasted, peeled and seeded

½ white onion, diced

1½ cups (6 oz/185 g) grated Manchego, mozzarella, Monterey Jack or other good melting cheese

½ cup (2 oz/60 g) grated Cotija, Romano or feta cheese

½ cup (2 oz/60 g) grated panela, dry cottage or dry ricotta cheese
   Freshly ground black pepper

12 small flour or corn tortillas, homemade *(recipes on pages 12–13)* or purchased, heated
   Green salsa *(recipe on page 14)*

☒ Preheat an oven to 375°F (190°C). Cut the poblano pepper and bell peppers lengthwise into strips 3 inches (7.5 cm) long and ¼ inch (6 mm) wide. Place in a bowl, add the onion and toss to mix. Set aside.

☒ In a separate bowl, combine all the cheeses and toss to mix. Set six 1-cup (8–fl oz/250-ml) or one 1½-qt (1.5-l) earthenware or glass baking dish in the oven to heat thoroughly, about 10 minutes.

☒ Distribute the cheeses evenly among the warmed small dishes or spread them evenly in the warmed large dish and return to the oven.

Cook for 5 minutes. Sprinkle the cheeses with the pepper-onion mixture and again return to the oven. Bake until the cheeses are completely melted and beginning to bubble, 5–7 minutes.

☒ Sprinkle with black pepper and serve immediately with warm tortillas and salsa on the side.

Serves 6

Beer-Battered Shrimp with Chipotle-Honey Sauce

Beer adds both flavor and texture to this lovely batter. If you make the batter early, it may thicken, in which case it can be thinned with a little more beer or with water. Too thick a batter will make the shrimp soggy, while a batter that is too thin won't form a complete coating.

BEER BATTER
1   cup (5 oz/155 g) all-purpose (plain) flour
1½ teaspoons cayenne pepper
1   teaspoon salt
1   teaspoon sugar
½   teaspoon baking powder
1   cup (8 fl oz/250 ml) beer

CHIPOTLE-HONEY
DIPPING SAUCE
2   dried chipotle chili peppers, stemmed and seeded
1   ripe tomato, quartered
½   small yellow onion, sliced
1   clove garlic
½   cup (4 fl oz/125 ml) water
1   teaspoon salt
¼   cup (3 fl oz/90 ml) honey
2   tablespoons red wine vinegar

Peanut oil for deep-frying
All-purpose (plain) flour for dusting
1¼ lb (625 g) rock shrimp or peeled white shrimp (prawns)

◈ To make the batter, in a bowl, combine the flour, cayenne, salt, sugar and baking powder. Stir to mix. Add the beer all at once and whisk until smooth. Set aside at room temperature for at least 30 minutes or up to 4 hours.

◈ To make the dipping sauce, in a small saucepan, combine the chilies, tomato, onion, garlic, water and salt and bring to a boil. Reduce the heat to low, cover and simmer gently until the ingredients soften and the mixture thickens, about 15 minutes. Remove from the heat and let cool slightly, then transfer to a blender and purée until smooth. Pour the purée into a small bowl and stir in the honey and vinegar. Let cool.

◈ In a large saucepan, pour in peanut oil to a depth of 5 inches (13 cm) and heat to 350°F (180°C) or until a few drops of batter sprinkled into the oil rise immediately to the surface. Spread some flour in a shallow bowl and toss the shrimp in it to coat evenly, tapping off any excess. Drop the shrimp, a few at a time, into the batter. Using tongs or your fingers, remove the shrimp from the batter, draining off the excess, and drop into the hot oil. Deep-fry until light golden and crisp, about 2 minutes. Using a slotted spoon, transfer to paper towels to drain.

◈ Arrange the shrimp on a warmed platter and serve immediately with the dipping sauce.

Serves 6

21

Melted Cheese-and-Bean Sandwiches with Fresh Salsa

You're likely to find these bubbly, open-faced sandwiches served for breakfast in Mexico City.
An excellent use for leftover beans, they also make a terrific lunch or a snack at any time of day.
Crusty Mexican rolls, called bolillos, *are ideal, but any French or Italian bread will do.*

SALSA FRESCA
2   large ripe tomatoes, seeded and diced
¼   red (Spanish) onion, finely diced
1   fresh jalapeño or serrano chili pepper, stemmed, seeded and finely diced
2   tablespoons coarsely chopped fresh cilantro (fresh coriander)
    Juice of ½ lime
½   teaspoon salt
    Freshly ground black pepper

6   *bolillos* or French or Italian rolls
1½ cups (12 fl oz/375 ml) refried black beans *(recipe on pages 14–15)*
1   cup (4 oz/125 g) grated Manchego, asadero, Monterey Jack or white Cheddar cheese, or a mixture

◙ Preheat a broiler (griller).

◙ To make the salsa, in a small bowl, stir together the tomatoes, onion, chili, cilantro, lime juice, salt and black pepper to taste. Set aside.

◙ Split each roll in half lengthwise and spread each cut side with a layer of beans ¼ inch (6 mm) thick. Sprinkle the cheese(s) evenly over the beans.

◙ Arrange the split rolls on a baking sheet and place in the broiler (griller) 4–6 inches (10–15 cm) below the heat source. Broil (grill) until the bread is crunchy, the cheeses are melted and the beans are bubbly, 6–8 minutes.

◙ Serve hot with the salsa on the side.

Serves 6

Guacamole

Mashed avocado is a common garnish for cantina dishes. Add salt, chili, lime and cilantro, and you have guacamole, a combination that takes its name from ahuacatl *(avocado) and* molli *(mixture), in the language of southern Mexico's Nahuatl Indians. This great dip is best made with dark, bumpy-skinned Hass avocados. Store with the pits resting in the guacamole to help prevent the dip from oxidizing.*

3 ripe avocados
1 fresh jalapeño chili pepper, stemmed, seeded and finely chopped
½ white onion, diced
¼ cup (⅓ oz/10 g) coarsely chopped fresh cilantro (fresh coriander)
Juice of 1 lime
½ teaspoon salt
Freshly ground black pepper
1 ripe tomato, seeded and diced (optional)
Lettuce leaf, optional
Corn tortilla chips

◙ Cut each avocado lengthwise into quarters, removing the pit. Peel off the skin and place the pulp in a bowl. Using a potato masher, spoon or your hand, mash lightly. Add the jalapeño, onion, cilantro, lime juice, salt, pepper to taste and the diced tomato, if using. Mix just until combined; chunks of avocado should remain visible.

◙ To serve, spoon the guacamole into a serving bowl or onto a plate lined with a lettuce leaf. If not serving immediately, poke the avocado pits down into the center of the mixture, cover tightly with plastic wrap and refrigerate for up to 4 hours. Serve chilled, accompanied by tortilla chips.

Serves 4–6

Mussel Ceviche Tostadas

Tostadas take their name from their bases of toasted—that is, crisply fried—tortillas. They are variously topped with beans, lettuce, cheeses and, often, poultry or meat. In coastal towns like Veracruz, however, seafood stars, particularly the "citrus-cooked" seafood known as ceviche, a dish that some food historians believe was introduced to Mexico from Asia by Spanish galleon traders.

3	lb (1.5 kg) mussels in the shell
1	cup (8 fl oz/250 ml) dry white wine
6	bay leaves
2	ripe tomatoes, seeded and diced
1	small red (Spanish) onion, diced
1	cup (5 oz/155 g) small Spanish green olives or other small green olives such as French picholines
3	tablespoons coarsely chopped fresh oregano
⅔	cup (5 fl oz/155 ml) good-quality tomato juice
⅓	cup (3 fl oz/80 ml) fresh orange juice
⅓	cup (3 fl oz/80 ml) fresh lime juice
¼	cup (2 fl oz/60 ml) fruity Spanish olive oil or other fruity olive oil
1	teaspoon salt
½	teaspoon freshly ground pepper
6–8	small corn tortillas, homemade *(recipe on page 13)* or purchased Vegetable oil for frying
1	ripe avocado, pitted, peeled and mashed

☒ Scrub the mussels under cool running water and pull off and discard their beards. Discard any mussels that do not close to the touch.

☒ In a wide sauté pan, combine the wine and bay leaves and bring to a boil. Add enough mussels to the pan to cover the bottom in a single layer; cover, reduce the heat to medium and cook until they open, 3–5 minutes. Using a slotted spoon, lift out the mussels and transfer to a bowl to cool. Cook the remaining mussels in batches in the same liquid, discarding any mussels that do not open. Reserve the cooking liquid for another use.

☒ Remove the mussels from their shells and place them in a nonaluminum bowl. Add the tomatoes, onion, olives, oregano, tomato and citrus juices, olive oil, salt and pepper and stir gently to mix. Cover and refrigerate for 1–2 hours to allow the flavors to blend.

☒ Meanwhile, pour oil to a depth of ½ inch (12 mm) in a small frying pan and heat to 375°F (190°C) on a deep-frying thermometer. Working with 1 tortilla at a time and using tongs, slip the tortilla into the oil and fry, turning once, until crispy but not browned, about 1 minute on each side. Let drain on paper towels while you fry the remaining tortillas.

☒ To serve, place the tortillas on individual plates. Divide the ceviche evenly among the tortillas, spooning it on top. Place a dollop of mashed avocado on each and serve.

Serves 6–8

Sea Bass Ceviche with Lime and Cilantro

You can adapt this wonderful ceviche to many kinds of fish and shellfish, including halibut, snapper, grouper or shrimp. Freshness is so prized in Mexico that it's common for ceviche aficionados to take chopped vegetables and lime juice along on the fishing boat to dress the catch almost the moment it's pulled from the water.

1   lb (500 g) sea bass fillet

¾   cup (6 fl oz/180 ml) fresh lime juice

1   large ripe tomato, seeded and diced

1   small red (Spanish) onion, finely diced

½   cup (¾ oz/20 g) coarsely chopped fresh cilantro (fresh coriander)

2   fresh jalapeño chili peppers, stemmed and sliced crosswise into thin circles

2   cups (16 fl oz/500 ml) bottled clam juice

1   teaspoon salt, or to taste
    Romaine (cos) lettuce leaves if serving in goblets, or leaf lettuce if serving in shallow soup bowls
    Corn tortilla chips

☒ Dice the sea bass into ½-inch (12-mm) cubes and place in a shallow glass or porcelain dish. Add ½ cup (4 fl oz/120 ml) of the lime juice and toss to coat evenly. Let marinate for 30–45 minutes.

☒ Drain the fish and return to the shallow dish. Add the tomato, onion, cilantro, chilies, clam juice, salt and the remaining ¼ cup (2 fl oz/60 ml) lime juice. Stir to mix well, then cover and refrigerate for 1–2 hours to allow the flavors to blend.

☒ Serve the ceviche in tall chilled goblets with spears of romaine and tortilla chips scattered along the edge. Or line shallow soup bowls with leaf lettuce leaves and spoon the ceviche on top. Surround the edges of the bowls with tortilla chips.

Serves 6

Roasted Onions Stuffed with Cheese

An elegant appetizer inspired by country cooking, these fragrant onions also go well as a side dish for spicy skirt steak. The richness and smooth texture of the cheese perfectly complements the sweetness and crunch of the onions. Be sure to roast the onions very slowly to develop their full flavor.

4 medium-large yellow sweet onions, unpeeled

1 tablespoon cumin seeds

½ cup (2 oz/60 g) grated asadero, Manchego, Monterey Jack or other good melting cheese

1 cup (4 oz/125 g) grated Cotija, Romano or other aged cheese

3 tablespoons sour cream

1 tablespoon balsamic vinegar

3 dashes of hot-pepper sauce such as Tabasco

½ teaspoon salt

½ teaspoon freshly ground pepper

Preheat a broiler (griller). Place the unpeeled onions in a small baking pan and cover with aluminum foil. Place in the broiler about 5 inches (13 cm) from the heat source and broil (grill), turning every 5–10 minutes, until charred on the outside and soft all the way through, about 1 hour. Remove from the broiler and set aside to cool. Set the oven temperature to 375°F (190°C).

Peel the onions carefully, keeping them intact and discarding the outer charred skin. Cut the onions in half crosswise and, using a finger, remove the centers, forming roasted onion "cups" with walls about ¾ inch (2 cm) thick; reserve the centers. Line the bottom of each onion cup with a piece of the removed roasted onion to prevent the filling from leaking out.

In a small frying pan over medium heat, toast the cumin seeds, shaking the pan frequently, until lightly browned and fragrant, 2–3 minutes. Transfer the seeds to a cutting board and chop coarsely. Chop the remaining removed onion pulp and place in a small bowl. Add both cheeses, sour cream, cumin seeds, vinegar, hot-pepper sauce, salt and pepper and stir to mix well.

Divide the cheese mixture evenly among the onion cups. Place on a baking sheet and bake until browned and bubbling, 15–20 minutes. Serve hot.

Serves 4

Chicken, Chili and Cheese Tamales

Some version of these steamed cornmeal packets are served in every region in Mexico.
Pack each tamale generously and don't worry if they ooze slightly during cooking.

FILLING

4 chicken breast halves

2 cups (16 fl oz/500 ml) chicken stock, or as needed

4 fresh poblano chili peppers, roasted, peeled and seeded *(see glossary, page 125),* then cut lengthwise into strips 2 inches (5 cm) wide

½ cup (4 fl oz/125 ml) green salsa *(recipe on page 14)*
  Salt and freshly ground black pepper

½ lb (250 g) panela, Manchego or Monterey Jack cheese, cut into thin strips ¼ inch (6 mm) thick and 2 inches (5 cm) long

TAMALE DOUGH

4 fresh poblano chili peppers, roasted, peeled and seeded

½ cup (4 fl oz/125 ml) green salsa

1 cup (8 fl oz/250 ml) chicken stock, reserved from making filling

1 teaspoon baking soda (bicarbonate of soda)

2½ teaspoons salt

1½ lb (750 g) prepared *masa* dough, chilled

½ cup (4 oz/125 g) lard or vegetable shortening, chilled

1 package (8 oz/250 g) dried corn husks, soaked in hot water for at least 2 hours
  Green salsa and *crema* or sour cream

To make the filling, place the chicken breasts in a saucepan and add stock to cover. Bring to a boil, reduce the heat to low and simmer, uncovered, until tender and opaque throughout, about 15 minutes. Using a slotted spoon, transfer the chicken to a plate to cool; reserve the stock for the tamale dough. Remove the meat from the chicken bones, discard the skin and, using your fingers, shred the meat into strips 2 inches (5 cm) long. Place in a bowl and add the chili strips, salsa and salt and black pepper to taste. Toss to mix and set aside with the cheese strips.

To make the dough, in a blender, combine 2 of the chilies, the salsa, reserved chicken stock, baking soda and salt. Blend until smooth. Set aside.

Place the *masa* dough in a bowl and, using an electric mixer set on medium speed, beat until light in texture, about 5 minutes. Slowly add the chicken stock mixture, beating until combined. Increase the speed to high and add the lard or shortening, 1 tablespoon at a time. Continue beating until light and fluffy, about 15 minutes total.

To make the tamales, drain the corn husks and pat dry. Spread 1 large or slightly overlap 2 small softened husks on a work surface, with the narrow end(s) pointing away from you. Leaving about 3 inches (7.5 cm) uncovered at the top and 1½ inches (4 cm) uncovered at the bottom, spread about 2½ tablespoons of the *masa* mixture over the center area of the husk(s). Place a spoonful of the chicken mixture on the *masa* and place 2 or 3 cheese strips on top. Fold one long side of the husk covered with *masa* over the chicken and cheese to enclose the filling completely in *masa* and then fold the opposite long side back over the center. Fold the top down and the bottom up, overlapping the ends. Tie a long shred of a corn husk around the center to secure the ends. Wrap in aluminum foil. Repeat with the remaining ingredients.

Line a large steamer rack with the remaining corn husks and arrange the wrapped tamales on it. Place the rack over (not touching) simmering water in a pan. Cover and steam until the husks pull away from the *masa* without sticking, about 1¼ hours, adding boiling water to the pan as needed to maintain the original level.

To serve, remove the foil and place 2 tamales on each plate. Serve the salsa and the *crema* or sour cream in bowls on the side. Let guests unwrap the husks.

Makes 12–14 tamales; serves 6–7

Swiss Chard Empanadas

The turnovers of Mexico, empanadas are stuffed with all kinds of vegetables, including squashes, mushrooms and the chard used here. Be sure to use plenty of chard and season it well. You'll want to make a large batch of empanadas when you have the time, then store them well wrapped in the freezer for up to several weeks.

EMPANADA DOUGH

2 cups (10 oz/315 g) all-purpose (plain) flour

½ cup (4 oz/125 g) lard or unsalted butter, chilled

2½ tablespoons unsalted butter, chilled

½ teaspoon salt
About ⅓ cup (3 fl oz/80 ml) ice water

SWISS CHARD FILLING

2 tablespoons olive oil

1 large white onion, diced

½ teaspoon salt

½ teaspoon freshly ground pepper

2 bunches Swiss chard (silverbeet), about 1 lb (500 g) total weight, trimmed, leaves cut into small pieces and stems cut into ½-inch (12-mm) dice

¾ cup (3 oz/90 g) grated Cotija, Romano or Parmesan cheese

¼ cup (1 oz/30 g) grated asadero, Manchego, Monterey Jack cheese or other good melting cheese
Squeeze of fresh lime juice

1 egg, beaten, for glaze
Freshly cracked pepper

☙ To make the dough, in a bowl, combine the flour, lard, butter and salt. Mix lightly with your fingers until the mixture forms pea-sized pieces. Using a fork, stir in the ice water, a little at a time, until a dough forms, and then knead lightly until it comes together in a ball. Wrap in plastic wrap and refrigerate for at least 1 hour or as long as overnight.

☙ To make the filling, in a large frying pan over medium heat, warm the olive oil. Add the onion, salt and pepper and sauté until the onion is soft and begins to turn lightly golden, 7–10 minutes. Add the chard stems and cook for 1–2 minutes. Then add the chard leaves and cook, stirring, until tender, 3–4 minutes. Transfer to a bowl and let cool. Add the cheeses and lime juice and mix well. Taste and adjust the seasonings.

☙ To assemble the empanadas, on a lightly floured board, roll out the dough about ⅛ inch (3 mm) thick. Using a 3-inch (7.5-cm) round cookie cutter, cut out 12 rounds. Place about 2 tablespoons of the filling on one-half of each round, leaving a ½-inch (12-mm) border. Dampen the edges of the dough with a little of the egg glaze, then fold the dough over to enclose the filling. Seal the edges by pressing firmly with the tines of a fork. Arrange the empanadas on a tray, cover with plastic wrap and chill for at least 30 minutes or up to 3 days before baking.

☙ Preheat an oven to 350°F (180°C). Place the empanadas on a baking sheet. Brush the tops with the egg glaze and sprinkle with cracked pepper. Using a sharp knife, cut 2 or 3 small slits in the top of each empanada to allow steam to escape.

☙ Bake until golden, about 30 minutes. Transfer to a rack to cool. Serve warm or at room temperature.

Makes twelve 3-inch (7.5-cm) empanadas; serves 6

Salads

With a climate ranging from the tropics to the subtropics, Mexico is a true cornucopia of fresh produce, and cooks take full advantage of this abundance. Buttery avocados, crisp jicama, tangy watercress, peppers and squashes in a kaleidoscope of colors, and many other riches of the farm and garden enliven the salads you are likely to find in the cantina.

As you might expect from a cuisine that makes the most of seasonal produce—and one that often springs up amidst the same market stalls as well—there is a delightfully impromptu feeling to many cantina salads. Such staples as rice and beans, for example, might be transformed into salads in an instant with the addition of a confetti of squashes or peppers and a simple oil-and-vinegar dressing. Or an array of bright-hued tropical fruits and blood oranges might be combined with crisp, white jicama, and the whole mixture thrown into sharp relief by hot chilies.

As the last example suggests, strong similarities exist between salads and fresh salsas. Indeed, you are likely to find many of the salads that follow offered as accompaniments to grilled meat, pork or chicken, offering their own lively counterpoints to the main course with every bite.

Parsley, Mint and Watercress Salad with Garlic

One of the most popular greens in Mexico, peppery watercress joins here with the fresh tastes of parsley and mint—an exotic and interesting combination that is also a good way to use up any excess herbs in your garden. Parboiling the garlic mellows its sharpness and heightens the earthy flavor and buttery consistency.

Regular table salt

1 head garlic, separated into cloves, peeled and thinly sliced

¾ cup (6 fl oz/180 ml) olive oil

3 tablespoons fresh lemon juice

1 teaspoon sea salt

½ teaspoon freshly ground pepper

1 large bunch fresh flat-leaf (Italian) parsley, about ¼ lb (125 g), stemmed

1 large bunch fresh mint, about ¼ lb (125 g), stemmed

2 bunches watercress, about 10 oz (315 g) total weight, stemmed

❧ Bring a small saucepan three-fourths full of water to a boil and add table salt to taste. Add the garlic and parboil for about 3 minutes to soften slightly and mellow the flavor. Drain and let cool.

❧ Place the cooled garlic in a small bowl and add the oil, lemon juice, sea salt and pepper. Whisk to dissolve the sea salt and form a dressing.

❧ In a salad bowl, combine the parsley, mint and watercress. Drizzle the dressing over the greens and toss to coat evenly. Serve immediately.

Serves 4–6

Grilled Vegetable Salad

Perfect for cookouts, this hearty salad can be started as soon as the coals warm up, leaving the vegetables to marinate while the main course cooks. Or you can make the salad a day ahead, as it will improve in flavor overnight. Almost any seasonal vegetable can be substituted for those suggested here.

2　red (Spanish) onions, unpeeled
¼　cup (2 fl oz/60 ml) red wine vinegar
1　teaspoon salt, or to taste
½　teaspoon freshly ground pepper
3　tablespoons coarsely chopped fresh oregano or marjoram
1　large clove garlic, minced
⅔　cup (5 fl oz/155 ml) olive oil
1　medium or 2 small Japanese eggplants (aubergines)
1　zucchini (courgette)
1　yellow crookneck squash
1　bulb fennel
1　large red bell pepper (capsicum), seeded, deribbed and quartered lengthwise
　Lettuce leaves

❧ Preheat a broiler (griller) or prepare a fire in a charcoal grill.

❧ If using a broiler, place the unpeeled onions in a small baking pan and cover with aluminum foil. Place the pan in the broiler or place the onions directly on the grill rack about 5 inches (13 cm) from the heat source. Broil or grill, turning every 5–10 minutes, until charred on the outside and soft throughout, about 1 hour if using a broiler or 20–30 minutes if using a grill. Remove from the broiler or grill rack; set aside to cool slightly.

❧ Meanwhile, in a small bowl, whisk together the vinegar, salt, pepper, oregano or marjoram and garlic. Slowly add the olive oil, whisking constantly.

❧ Trim the ends from the eggplant(s) and squashes and any stalks from the fennel bulb and cut lengthwise into quarters. Place in a bowl with the bell pepper and half of the vinaigrette and toss to mix. Arrange the vegetables on a broiler pan or directly on the grill rack about 5 inches (13 cm) from the heat source. Broil or grill slowly, turning to cook evenly, until lightly golden and cooked through, 5–10 minutes for the squashes, peppers and eggplants and 15 minutes for the fennel. Remove from the broiler or grill rack and let cool slightly.

❧ Peel the onions and cut into 2-inch (5-cm) pieces. Place in a bowl. Cut all the remaining vegetables into 2-inch (5-cm) pieces as well and add to the bowl. Pour the remaining vinaigrette over the vegetables and toss well to coat.

❧ To serve, line individual plates with lettuce leaves and spoon the vegetables on top.

Serves 4–6

Avocado and Tomatillo Salad

This home-style salad showcases the wonderful contrasts present when rich, creamy avocado,
sharp-tasting tomatillos and crunchy croutons come together. The vegetables must be at their peak of ripeness
for the best results. The avocado should be only slightly soft, so it holds up during tossing.

½ cup (4 fl oz/120 ml) olive oil

⅓ loaf crusty French, Italian or sourdough bread, cut into ¾-inch (2-cm) cubes

   Salt to taste, plus 1 teaspoon

   Freshly ground pepper to taste, plus ½ teaspoon

2 ripe avocados, pitted, peeled and cut into ¾-inch (2-cm) cubes

2 cups (12 oz/375 g) red or yellow cherry tomatoes, or a mixture, halved

2 bunches fresh cilantro (fresh coriander), about 6 oz (185 g) total weight, stemmed

5 tomatillos, husked and quartered

1 tablespoon fresh lime juice

2 tablespoons distilled white or white wine vinegar

   Lettuce leaves

6 green (spring) onions, thinly sliced

❧ In a frying pan over medium heat, warm ¼ cup (2 fl oz/60 ml) of the olive oil. Add the bread cubes and shake the pan to coat the cubes lightly on all sides. Sprinkle with salt and pepper to taste, reduce the heat to medium-low and toast, shaking the pan occasionally, until golden brown on all sides, about 15 minutes. Remove from the heat and let cool.

❧ In a bowl, combine the avocados, cherry tomatoes and cilantro; set aside. In a blender or a food processor fitted with the metal blade, combine the tomatillos, lime juice, vinegar, the remaining ¼ cup (2 fl oz/ 60 ml) olive oil, the 1 teaspoon salt and the ½ teaspoon pepper. Blend well to form a smooth dressing.

❧ Pour the dressing over the avocado mixture and begin to toss lightly to mix. When almost fully mixed, add the croutons and continue to toss until all the ingredients are evenly distributed.

❧ To serve, line a platter or individual salad bowls with lettuce leaves and spoon the avocado mixture on top. Garnish with the green onions and serve immediately.

Serves 4–6

Jicama and Blood Orange Salad

Throughout Mexico, you'll find jicama—a crisp, refreshing, white-fleshed root vegetable—eaten raw as a snack, sprinkled with chili powder. Natives of the Yucatán peninsula also enjoy it paired with exotic fruit in salads such as this one, which features red-fleshed blood oranges. Try this chopped as a salsa for grilled fish, too.

1   jicama, about ¾ lb (375 g)

3   blood oranges

1   papaya (pawpaw) or mango or ¼ pineapple

1   small red (Spanish) onion, thinly sliced

1   teaspoon sea salt

¼   dried habanero chili pepper, seeded and finely chopped or ground to a powder, or cayenne pepper to taste (optional)

3   tablespoons olive oil

    Juice of 1 lime

1   bunch fresh cilantro (fresh coriander), about 3 oz (90 g), stemmed

1   bunch fresh mint, about 3 oz (90 g), stemmed

❧ Using a paring knife, peel the jicama, including the fibrous layer just beneath the skin. Thinly slice the flesh and then cut into thin strips 2 inches (5 cm) long and ¼ inch (6 mm) thick. Place in a large bowl.

❧ Working with 1 orange at a time and using a sharp knife, cut a slice off the top and bottom of the oranges to reveal the fruit. Place each orange upright on a cutting board and cut away the peel and any white membrane. Then, holding the orange over the bowl with the jicama, cut along either side of each segment to free it, letting the segments and any juices fall into the bowl. If using a papaya, halve lengthwise, scoop out and discard the seeds and peel the halves. If using a mango, peel it and cut the flesh from the pit. If using pineapple,

cut away the peel and the tough core area. Cut the papaya, mango or pineapple into ½-inch (12-mm) dice; you should have about 1½ cups (9 oz/ 280 g). Add to the bowl.

❧ Add the onion, salt, habanero chili or cayenne pepper, olive oil, lime juice, cilantro and mint to the bowl. Toss gently to mix. Cover and refrigerate for 2 hours before serving.

Serves 4–6

Three Beans and Three Peppers Salad

Two Mexican pantry staples—beans and peppers—are featured here, with three different varieties of each playing the central roles. Start testing the beans for doneness early, as cooking times vary greatly with age and variety.

½ cup (3½ oz/105 g) dried black beans

½ cup (3½ oz/105 g) dried pinto beans

½ cup (3½ oz/105 g) dried red or kidney beans

1 yellow bell pepper (capsicum)

1 red bell pepper (capsicum)

1 fresh poblano chili pepper

¼ cup (2 fl oz/60 ml) red wine vinegar

1 teaspoon salt

½ teaspoon freshly ground black pepper

1 canned chipotle chili pepper in vinegar or in *adobo* sauce, stemmed, seeded and minced (optional)

⅔ cup (5 fl oz/160 ml) olive oil

1 red (Spanish) onion, finely diced

☙ Sort through all the beans, keeping them separate, and discard any misshapen beans or stones. Rinse well. Place each bean variety in a separate saucepan and add water to cover generously. Bring each to a boil, reduce the heat to medium-low, cover and simmer until the smallest bean is cooked through and creamy inside, about 1½ hours. Drain all the beans in a colander (they can be mixed at this time) and spread them out on a plate to cool slightly.

☙ Meanwhile, remove the stems, seeds and ribs from the bell peppers and poblano chili. Cut the peppers into ¼-inch (6-mm) dice, or a size as similar as possible to that of the cooked beans. In a large bowl, whisk together the vinegar, salt, black pepper and chipotle chili, if using. Slowly add the olive oil, whisking constantly. Toss in the diced peppers, onion and warm beans and mix well.

☙ Cover and refrigerate for at least 2 hours or as long as overnight. Serve the salad chilled.

Serves 4–6

Summer Squash and Rice Salad

A cantina cook might throw together a salad much like this one to use up leftovers. The mixture of rice and vegetables yields a balanced flavor and texture that doesn't become soggy. Success depends upon cooking and seasoning everything separately so the flavors remain pronounced when the ingredients are combined.

8   tablespoons (4 fl oz/125 ml)
    olive oil
5   assorted small summer squashes
    such as zucchini (courgettes),
    yellow crookneck or straightneck,
    or pattypan, in any combination,
    trimmed and cut into ¼-inch
    (6-mm) dice
    Salt and freshly ground pepper
1   yellow onion, diced
2   cloves garlic, crushed
2   teaspoons ground cumin
2   tablespoons distilled white or
    cider vinegar
2   cups (14 oz/440 g) steamed rice
    (recipe on page 15), cooled to room
    temperature
½   cup (¾ oz/20 g) coarsely chopped
    fresh parsley
    Chopped lettuce leaves

❧ In a frying pan over high heat, warm 2 tablespoons of the olive oil. Add one-third each of the squashes and season to taste with salt and pepper. Sauté, stirring often, until lightly browned and slightly soft, 1–2 minutes. Transfer to a bowl. Cook the remaining squashes, in 2 batches, in the same way, using 2 tablespoons oil with each batch. Let the squashes cool.

❧ In the same frying pan, heat the remaining 2 tablespoons oil over medium heat. Add the onion and sauté until lightly golden, 3–5 minutes. Stir in the garlic and cook briefly. Add the cumin, reduce the heat to low and sauté for about 2 minutes

longer. Add to the bowl holding the squashes. Add the vinegar, rice and parsley and toss to mix well. Taste and adjust the seasonings. (At this point, the salad can be covered and refrigerated for up to 3 days. Bring to room temperature before serving.)

❧ To serve, line individual plates with lettuce leaves and spoon the salad on top.

Serves 4–6

Tropical Green Salad

Pumpkin seeds, known in Spanish as pepitas, *have been part of the Mexican pantry since
before the arrival of Columbus in the New World, while pomegranate seeds came to the Americas with
the Spanish conquistadores. Here these two distinctive ingredients are joined by the musky papaya,
a Caribbean native, in a colorful salad that complements simple grilled poultry and meats.*

ORANGE-SHALLOT DRESSING
3   tablespoons red wine vinegar
1   tablespoon fresh orange juice
3   small shallots, minced
1   teaspoon salt
½   teaspoon freshly ground pepper
6   tablespoons (3 fl oz/90 ml)
    extra-virgin olive oil

½   cup (2½ oz/75 g) raw hulled
    green pumpkin seeds
1   tablespoon soy sauce
1   pomegranate
1   ripe papaya (pawpaw)
3   small bunches baby arugula
    (rocket), stemmed, carefully
    washed and dried
1   cup (5 oz/155 g) crumbled
    Cabrales or Roquefort cheese

☙ To make the dressing, in a small bowl, whisk together the vinegar, orange juice, shallots, salt and pepper until the salt dissolves. Add the olive oil in a slow stream, whisking constantly until emulsified. Set aside.

☙ In a small, dry frying pan over medium heat, toast the pumpkin seeds until slightly puffed and golden, 3–5 minutes. Add the soy sauce and stir to mix, then immediately remove from the heat. Turn the pumpkin seeds onto a plate to cool.

☙ Cut off the blossom end of the pomegranate, removing some of the membrane but not cutting into the seeds. Score the skin into quarters, then break the fruit apart gently, following the scored lines. Bend back the thin hard skin and pull the seeds free of it. (If this step is done in a basin of water, the membrane and skin will float and the seeds will sink.) Set the seeds aside.

☙ Cut the papaya in half lengthwise and scoop out and discard the seeds. Cut each half into thin slices and place in a large salad bowl.

☙ Add the arugula, cheese and pomegranate seeds to the papaya. Drizzle on just enough of the dressing to coat, then toss gently. Sprinkle the pumpkin seeds over the top and serve. Pass the remaining dressing at the table.

Serves 4

Soups and Stews

Cantinas at their most basic—those that serve only one simple dish—will in all likelihood offer a soup or a stew. Nothing could be easier to make: just simmer some vegetables, beans, meat, poultry or seafood in a stock that you've made from flavorful vegetables and bones or trimmings, and the result is a satisfying feast in a bowl.

Many soups and stews typify the thrifty nature of cantina cooking. Tortilla soup and *chilaquiles,* for example, make delicious use of leftover corn tortillas; garlic soup draws complex flavor from a humble seasoning; and chili and the popular meatballs known as albóndigas feature economical ground poultry and meat. Not surprisingly given their central role in the Mexican diet, beans feature in some of the recipes, offering their own earthy satisfaction.

As you look through the recipes on the pages that follow, you will find the stews distinguished from the soups by their heartier, thicker texture and the frequent addition of meat, poultry or seafood. But the border between the two is hazy, and either one, accompanied with tortillas or bread and, perhaps, a salad, can easily become the centerpiece of a meal.

Green Gazpacho

*This variation on a traditional Spanish soup is lively and refreshing. You'll
want to serve it ice cold on the hottest of days or before a hearty meal. Simply prepared
cheese quesadillas or lightly salted breadsticks make a lovely accompaniment.*

2 slices day-old white bread, crusts removed

1 celery stalk, including leaves, chopped

6 tomatillos, husked and chopped

1 small green bell pepper (capsicum), seeded, deribbed and cut up

2 large or 6 small pickling cucumbers, peeled and cut up

1 fresh jalapeño chili pepper, stemmed, seeded (if desired) and cut up

3 cloves garlic, cut up

1 teaspoon salt
 Juice of 1 lime

¼ cup (⅓ oz/10 g) coarsely chopped fresh cilantro (fresh coriander)

2 cups (16 fl oz/500 ml) vegetable stock or water

MAYONNAISE

2 egg yolks

2 tablespoons tarragon vinegar

1½ teaspoons salt

½ teaspoon freshly ground black pepper

⅔ cup (5 fl oz/155 ml) olive oil

 Chopped fresh chives

½ small avocado, peeled and sliced

☜ Place the slices of bread in a shallow bowl and add water to cover. Let stand for 5 minutes, then squeeze the bread dry. Set aside.

☜ In a food processor fitted with the metal blade, combine the celery, tomatillos, bell pepper, cucumbers, jalapeño chili, the bread, garlic, salt, lime juice and cilantro. Process until finely puréed. Working in batches, transfer to a blender with the vegetable stock or water and purée until smooth. Set aside.

☜ To make the mayonnaise, in a large bowl, whisk together the egg yolks, vinegar, salt and pepper. Gradually add the olive oil, drop by drop, whisking until an emulsion forms. As the mixture thickens, you can begin adding the oil more quickly. (If the mayonnaise becomes overly thick or looks stringy, add 1 tablespoon water and then continue.)

☜ Once all the oil has been added and the mayonnaise is thick, start adding the vegetable purée, ¼ cup (2 fl oz/60 ml) at a time, whisking constantly, until thoroughly blended. Taste and adjust the seasonings. Cover and chill for at least 2 hours or up to 24 hours.

☜ Ladle into chilled bowls. Sprinkle with chopped chives and top each serving with a slice of avocado.

Serves 4–6

Pork and Hominy in a Red Chile Broth

Pozole is a staple of the Mexican table, and each region offers several variations.
The stew's name refers to whole-kernel hominy—large kernels of dried corn that have been
soaked in unslaked lime to remove their outer skins and puff them up. In this recipe, tougher cuts
like pork shoulder or butt give abundant flavor and grow tender with slow, gentle cooking.

1 lb (500 g) boneless stewing pork, cut into 1-inch (2.5-cm) cubes
½ teaspoon salt
4 cups (32 fl oz/1 l) water
4 dried ancho chili peppers, stemmed and seeded
5 cloves garlic
1½ teaspoons dried oregano
2 tablespoons vegetable oil
1 large yellow onion, diced
2 cups (12 oz/375 g) well-drained canned hominy
3 cups (24 fl oz/750 ml) chicken or pork stock, or as needed
Sliced radishes, shredded lettuce, diced yellow onion, corn tortilla chips, diced avocado and lime wedges for garnish

~ In a sauté pan, combine the pork cubes and salt with the water. Bring to a boil, reduce the heat to medium and simmer gently, uncovered, until barely tender, about 20 minutes. Remove from the heat and let the pork cool in the liquid. Drain, reserving the liquid in a bowl. Set the meat aside, covering it with a damp towel.

~ Place the ancho chilies in the reserved warm cooking liquid and let soak for 20 minutes. Transfer the liquid and chilies to a blender. Add the garlic and oregano and purée until smooth. Set aside.

~ In a heavy saucepan over medium-high heat, warm the vegetable oil. Add the onion and sauté until lightly golden, about 10 minutes. Add the puréed chili mixture, hominy and chicken or pork stock, adding more stock if needed for a more soupy consistency. Stir in the reserved pork. Bring to a boil, reduce the heat to medium-low and simmer gently, uncovered, until the pork is fork-tender, about 30 minutes. Taste and adjust the seasonings.

~ Ladle the stew into warmed shallow bowls. Arrange the garnishes in small bowls and let guests add to the stew to taste.

Serves 4–6

Cream of Chayote Soup

Related to squashes and cucumbers, mild-flavored chayotes—sometimes called vegetable pears—are believed to be indigenous to Mexico and are grown throughout the country. The most common variety, pale green and about the size and shape of a large pear, are used in this soup. If you can't find them, substitute zucchini (courgettes), which approximate the flavor, or use cauliflower or kohlrabi.

1   large slice bacon or 2 tablespoons unsalted butter

1   yellow onion, diced

1   teaspoon salt

½   teaspoon freshly ground pepper

5   cups (40 fl oz/1.25 l) chicken stock, vegetable stock or water

2   bay leaves

1   small boiling potato, peeled and sliced

4   chayotes, peeled, seeded and sliced

1   cup (8 fl oz/250 ml) heavy (double) cream or half-and-half (half cream)

2   limes, thinly sliced

In a large soup pot over low heat, fry the bacon until almost all the fat is rendered, or melt the butter. Raise the heat to medium, add the onion, salt and pepper and cook, stirring occasionally, until soft, about 5 minutes. Add the stock or water, bay leaves and potato and simmer until the potato slices are soft, about 20 minutes.

When the potato slices are soft, remove and discard the bay leaves and bacon. Add the chayotes and bring to a boil. Return the heat to medium and simmer, uncovered, until the chayotes are soft, about 15 minutes.

Remove from the heat and let cool slightly. Working in batches, purée the soup in a blender until smooth. As each batch is puréed, pour the purée through a sieve placed over a bowl, pressing with the back of a spoon to extract all the juices. Pour the purée back into the pot, add the cream or half-and-half and bring just to a boil. Taste and adjust the seasonings.

Remove from the heat and ladle into warmed bowls. Slip a few lime slices into each bowl and serve hot.

Serves 6

Sea Bass Veracruzana

*Seaside restaurants in Veracruz regularly feature fish cooked with onion, garlic,
chilies and tomatoes. Sea bass, which takes well to searing and cooks evenly without flaking,
makes a good choice. Be sure to get the pan very hot before adding the fish.*

1½ lb (750 g) sea bass or other firm-fleshed fish fillets, cut into 4 equal portions
Salt and freshly ground pepper

3 tablespoons olive oil

1 small yellow onion, thinly sliced

2 cloves garlic, minced

2 fresh jalapeño chili peppers, stemmed and cut into rounds ¼ inch (6 mm) thick

1 lime, cut into 8 wedges

1 ripe tomato, seeded and cut into strips

1½ tablespoons coarsely chopped fresh oregano

½ cup (2½ oz/75 g) small Spanish green olives or other small green olives such as French picholines, pitted

½ cup (4 fl oz/125 ml) dry white wine

¾ cup (6 fl oz/180 ml) fish stock or bottled clam juice

☢ Sprinkle the fish fillets on both sides with salt and pepper. Heat 1 very large or 2 medium-sized sauté pans over medium-high heat for 1 minute. Add the olive oil and when it is hot but not smoking, add the fish fillets, skin side up. Turn the heat to high and sear the fillets on the first side until golden brown, 1–2 minutes. Turn and sear on the second side, 1–2 minutes longer. Remove from the heat.

☢ Using a slotted spatula, transfer the fillets to a rack set over a plate to catch the juices. Return the pan(s) to high heat, add the onion and sauté, stirring often, until lightly golden, 2–3 minutes. Add the garlic, jalapeños, lime wedges, tomato, oregano and olives and sauté, stirring briskly, for 1 minute longer. Add the white wine and boil until reduced by half, 2–3 minutes. Add the fish stock or clam juice and bring to a boil.

Reduce the heat to medium-low and return the fish fillets along with their juices to the pan(s). Cover and simmer gently until opaque throughout, 1–3 minutes depending upon the thickness of the fillets.

☢ Taste the broth and adjust the seasonings. Using the spatula, transfer the fish to warmed shallow soup bowls. Ladle the broth into the bowls, arranging some of the vegetables from the broth on the top of each fillet. Serve immediately.

Serves 4

Poached Eggs in Roasted Tomato Broth

Morning meals in cantinas often feature brothy dishes like this one, which can also double as a light midday repast or dinner in summertime. Mexican cooks sometimes call this simple preparation huevos ahogados, or "drowned eggs." Be sure to roast the tomatoes until uniformly charred, to develop a smoky flavor.

4 tomatoes

4 cups (32 fl oz/1 l) chicken stock

2 tablespoons olive oil

1 yellow onion, thinly sliced

1 teaspoon salt

½ teaspoon freshly ground black pepper

3 cloves garlic, minced

2 fresh serrano chili peppers

8 eggs

¼ cup (1 oz/30 g) grated Cotija, Romano or Parmesan cheese

4 large flour tortillas, homemade *(recipe on page 12)* or purchased, heated

☒ Preheat a broiler (griller). Place the tomatoes in a shallow baking pan and place in the broiler 4–6 inches (10–15 cm) from the heat source. Broil (grill), turning occasionally, until charred on all sides, 10–12 minutes.

☒ Remove the tomatoes from the broiler, let cool slightly and cut out the cores. Transfer to a blender, add 1 cup (8 fl oz/250 ml) of the chicken stock and purée until smooth. Set aside.

☒ In a heavy, wide saucepan or deep sauté pan over medium heat, warm the olive oil. When it is nearly smoking, add the onion, salt and pepper and sauté until golden brown, about 15 minutes. Add the garlic and whole serrano chilies and sauté for 1 minute longer. Add the tomato purée and the remaining 3 cups (24 fl oz/ 750 ml) chicken stock and bring to a boil. Reduce the heat to medium and simmer, uncovered, for 10 minutes to blend the flavors.

☒ To poach the eggs, one at a time, crack them into a cup and gently slide them into the simmering broth. Cook the eggs, basting the tops occasionally with spoonfuls of the hot broth, until the whites are set but the yolks are still soft, 4–6 minutes.

☒ Using a slotted spoon, gently lift out the eggs and place 2 in each warmed soup bowl. Ladle the broth over the eggs and garnish with the grated cheese. Serve immediately with the flour tortillas alongside.

Serves 4

Albóndigas Soup with Cilantro Pesto

Taking its name from the word for the meatballs that float in its rich broth, this great one-dish meal is arguably the national soup of Mexico. Make a big pot for a casual party, keeping it warm on the stove top. Adding the cilantro pesto to each serving produces a wonderfully fresh taste.

¾ cup (5½ oz/170 g) short-grain white rice

1½ cups (12 fl oz/375 ml) water

4 tablespoons (2 fl oz/60 ml) vegetable oil

2 white onions, diced

½ lb (250 g) ground (minced) pork

½ lb (250 g) ground (minced) beef

1 egg

1 teaspoon ground cumin

1 teaspoon dried oregano

1½ teaspoons salt

1 teaspoon freshly ground pepper

1 clove garlic, minced

1 zucchini (courgette), diced

2 carrots, peeled and diced

2 ripe tomatoes, peeled, seeded and diced

6 cups (48 fl oz/1.5 l) chicken stock

CILANTRO PESTO

½ cup (¾ oz/20 g) coarsely chopped fresh cilantro (fresh coriander)

1 fresh mint sprig, stemmed and chopped

Juice of 2 limes

2 tablespoons olive oil

2 tablespoons water

½ teaspoon salt

☙ Place the rice in a heatproof bowl. Bring the water to a boil and pour it over the rice. Let soak for 40 minutes, then drain; set aside.

☙ Meanwhile, in a sauté pan over medium heat, warm 2 tablespoons of the vegetable oil. Add 1 of the onions and sauté until soft, about 5 minutes. Remove from the heat and let cool.

☙ In a bowl, combine the pork, beef, cooled onion, soaked rice, egg, cumin, oregano, ¾ teaspoon of the salt and ½ teaspoon of the pepper. Using your hands, mix well and form into 1-inch (2.5-cm) balls.

☙ In a large soup pot over medium heat, warm the remaining 2 tablespoons vegetable oil. Add the remaining onion and sauté until soft, about 5 minutes. Add the garlic, zucchini, carrots and tomatoes and cook, stirring, until fragrant, about 5 minutes. Add the chicken stock, stir well and bring to a boil. Carefully slip the meatballs into the pot, reduce the heat to low and simmer uncovered until the meatballs are fully cooked, about 45 minutes. Stir in the remaining ¾ teaspoon salt and ½ teaspoon pepper.

☙ While the soup simmers, make the cilantro pesto: In a mini food processor or a blender, combine the cilantro, mint, lime juice, olive oil, water and salt. Process to a paste.

☙ Ladle the soup into warmed soup bowls and top each serving with a dollop of cilantro pesto. Serve at once.

Serves 6–8

Turkey Black Bean Chili with Ancho Salsa

Some food scholars say that chili-seasoned stews of meat and beans belong more to Texas and the American Southwest than to Mexico. Certainly, this is a cantina dish of the northern borderlands, and it owes a debt to present-day sensibilities in its health-conscious combination of ground turkey and black beans.

2   cups (14 oz/440 g) dried black beans
8   cups (64 fl oz/2 l) water
2   fresh árbol chili peppers
3   bay leaves

ANCHO SALSA
4   dried ancho chili peppers, stemmed and seeded
½   cup (4 fl oz/125 ml) fresh orange juice
¼   cup (2 fl oz/60 ml) fresh lime juice
1   teaspoon salt
2   tablespoons extra-virgin olive oil

2   tablespoons vegetable oil
1   lb (500 g) coarsely ground (minced) turkey
1   large yellow onion, diced
1   teaspoon salt, or to taste
½   teaspoon freshly ground black pepper
½   teaspoon cayenne pepper
3   cloves garlic, minced
2   fresh poblano chili peppers, stemmed, seeded and diced
1½   tablespoons chili powder
1½   tablespoons ground cumin
2   cups (16 fl oz/500 ml) chicken stock, or as needed

Sort through the black beans and discard any misshapen beans or stones. Rinse well. In a large saucepan, combine the beans, water, árbol chilies and bay leaves and bring to a boil. Reduce the heat to medium, cover and simmer until tender, about 1 hour. Remove the chilies and bay leaves and discard. Set aside.

Meanwhile, make the salsa: In a cast-iron frying pan over medium heat, toast the ancho chilies, turning frequently to avoid scorching, until soft and brown, 1–2 minutes. Remove from the heat, chop and place in a bowl. Add the orange and lime juices, salt and olive oil. Mix well and let stand at room temperature for at least 30 minutes or up to 2 hours before serving. (The salsa can be covered and refrigerated for up to 2 days.)

In a large pot over medium heat, warm the vegetable oil. Add the turkey and cook, stirring often, until browned, about 10 minutes. Add the onion, salt, black pepper and cayenne pepper and sauté over medium heat, stirring occasionally, until lightly golden, about 10 minutes. Add the garlic, poblano chilies, chili powder and cumin and cook, stirring, until fragrant, 2–3 minutes. Add the black beans and their liquid and the 2 cups (16 fl oz/500 ml) chicken stock and cook, uncovered, until the flavors have blended and the mixture has thickened, 30–40 minutes. Taste and adjust the seasonings, adding more chicken stock if needed for the desired consistency.

Ladle the chili into warmed bowls and top each serving with a dollop of the salsa.

Serves 6

Saffron Mussel Stew

You find a lot of Spanish influence in the Yucatán region, where this classic stew originates. The presence of saffron is evidence of Spain's contribution to many of the area's dishes. Serve with a tossed green salad and generous slices of broiled garlic bread.

2 tablespoons olive oil

2 yellow onions, cut into julienne strips

½ teaspoon salt

½ teaspoon freshly ground pepper

4 cloves garlic, sliced

1½ cups (12 fl oz/375 ml) dry white wine

1 fresh thyme sprig

1 teaspoon saffron threads

2½ cups (20 fl oz/625 ml) bottled clam juice or fish stock

1 cup (8 fl oz/250 ml) good-quality tomato juice

3 lb (1.5 kg) small mussels in the shell

½ cup (¾ oz/20 g) coarsely chopped fresh flat-leaf (Italian) parsley

✎ In a large, heavy-bottomed saucepan over medium heat, warm 1 tablespoon of the olive oil. Add half of the onions, salt and pepper and sauté, stirring briskly, until lightly golden, 8–10 minutes. Add the garlic and sauté for 1 minute longer. Then add the white wine and bring to a boil. Boil until reduced by half, 7–8 minutes. Add the thyme, saffron, clam juice or fish stock and tomato juice and bring to a boil. Reduce the heat to low and simmer for 10 minutes to blend the flavors. Strain through a sieve into a bowl and set aside.

✎ Scrub the mussels under cool running water and pull out and discard their beards. Discard any mussels that do not close to the touch.

✎ Place 2 large, wide sauté pans over high heat (or work in batches if only 1 pan is available). Add half of the remaining 1 tablespoon olive oil to each pan. When hot, add half of the remaining onions to each pan and sauté briefly, stirring occasionally, until they just begin to color, about 4 minutes. Add half of the mussels to each pan, spreading them out in a single layer, and sauté, stirring occasionally, for 1–2 minutes. Add half of the strained broth to each pan and bring to a boil. Immediately reduce the heat to medium, cover and cook until all the mussels open, 3–5 minutes. Discard any mussels that do not open.

✎ Add half of the parsley to each pan. Toss to mix and then spoon the mussels into warmed shallow soup bowls. Divide the broth evenly among the bowls and serve immediately.

Serves 4

Garlic Soup

Although garlic originally came to Mexico with the Spanish explorers, it is now so ubiquitous that this soup regularly turns up on lunch menus in casual restaurants there. Do not be put off by the amount of garlic; the flavor mellows and sweetens with slow cooking. With its straight-forward flavors and intriguing textures, this makes an ideal first course for a grand feast.

3 tablespoons mild olive oil

9 cloves garlic, halved

½ loaf crusty French bread, cut into 1-inch (2.5-cm) cubes (2 generous cups/5 oz/155 g)

1 teaspoon salt

½ teaspoon freshly ground pepper

8 cups (64 fl oz/2 l) chicken stock

3 eggs, lightly beaten

2 tablespoons fresh epazote or oregano leaves, chopped

1 lime, cut into 6 wedges

☙ Preheat an oven to 325°F (165°C). In a soup pot over low heat, warm the olive oil. Add the garlic and cook slowly, stirring occasionally, until the oil is well flavored and the garlic is soft but has not begun to color, about 5 minutes. Remove from the heat and discard the garlic cloves.

☙ Place the bread cubes in a bowl and pour about half of the garlicky oil over them (leave the remaining oil in the pot). Toss well to coat, sprinkle with the salt and pepper, and spread out on a baking sheet. Bake until golden brown and crisp throughout, 10–15 minutes. Remove from the oven and set aside.

☙ Pour the stock into the soup pot holding the remaining oil. Place over medium heat and bring to a simmer.

Gradually add the eggs to the simmering stock while stirring the stock constantly in a circular motion. Add the epazote or oregano and simmer until the eggs are set, about 3 minutes longer. Remove from the heat.

☙ Divide the croutons among 6 warmed soup bowls and ladle the egg-laced stock into them. Squeeze a wedge of lime over each bowl, then drop the wedge in the bowl. Serve immediately.

Serves 6

Red Chicken and Tortilla Soup

The most common use for leftover tortillas throughout Mexico, chilaquiles *are essentially pieces of stale tortilla cooked or softened in chili sauce. Depending upon the cantina, this can translate into cheesy casseroles, thick porridges or brothy soups. This version relies on red salsa, but green can be substituted.*

6   cups (48 fl oz/1.5 l) chicken
    stock
1   lb (500 g) skinless, boneless
    chicken breasts
    Salt to taste, plus 1 teaspoon
    Freshly ground pepper to taste,
    plus ½ teaspoon
2   tablespoons vegetable oil
1   yellow onion, diced
3   cloves garlic, minced
2   cups (16 fl oz/500 ml) red salsa
    (recipe on page 14)
1   cup (8 fl oz/250 ml) water
2   handfuls corn tortilla chips

GARNISHES
¼   cup (⅓ oz/10 g) coarsely chopped
    fresh cilantro (fresh coriander)
¼   yellow onion, diced
¼   cup (1 oz/30 g) grated Cotija,
    Romano or Parmesan cheese
¼   cup (2 fl oz/60 ml) *crema* or
    sour cream

☒ In a deep frying pan, bring the chicken stock to a boil. Sprinkle the chicken breasts with salt and pepper to taste and add to the stock. Reduce the heat to medium, cover and cook until tender and opaque throughout, 8–10 minutes. Using a slotted spoon, remove the chicken breasts, wrap in a damp towel and set aside to cool. Reserve the stock.

☒ In a large saucepan over medium heat, warm the vegetable oil. Add the onion, 1 teaspoon salt and ½ teaspoon pepper and sauté until soft, about 5 minutes. Add the garlic and sauté until soft but not browned, 2–3 minutes longer. Add the salsa, reserved chicken stock and water. Bring to a boil over high heat, reduce the heat to medium and simmer, uncovered, for 10 minutes to blend the flavors.

☒ Using your fingers, shred the cooled chicken meat into long, thin strips. Add to the pan along with the tortilla chips. Stir well, taste and adjust the seasonings. Continue to simmer over medium heat for 3–4 minutes to soften the chips slightly. The chips should still be half crispy.

☒ Ladle the soup into warmed soup bowls. Garnish each serving with cilantro, onion, cheese and a spoonful of *crema* or sour cream. Serve immediately.

Serves 4–6

Pinto Bean Soup with Fresh Salsa

Despite its creamy taste, this simply prepared soup is surprisingly low in fat. A cantina cook might well make up a batch from the previous day's leftover beans. It is the perfect antidote to a blustery day, and the fresh, sharp garnish contrasts nicely with the natural richness of the beans.

1½ cups (10½ oz/330 g) dried pinto beans
7 cups (56 fl oz/1.75 l) water
¼ cup (2 fl oz/60 ml) vegetable oil
2 yellow onions, diced
1 teaspoon salt
½ teaspoon freshly ground pepper
4 cloves garlic, minced
6 cups (48 fl oz/1.5 l) chicken stock, vegetable stock or water

SALSA
3 ripe plum (Roma) tomatoes, diced
½ small red (Spanish) onion, finely diced
¼ cup (⅓ oz/10 g) coarsely chopped fresh cilantro (fresh coriander)
    Juice of 1 lime
    Salt and freshly ground pepper

Crema or sour cream

◈ Sort through the beans and discard any misshapen beans or stones. Rinse well. Place the beans in a saucepan and add the water. Bring to a boil, reduce the heat to medium-low, cover and simmer until the smallest bean is cooked through and creamy inside, about 1½ hours. Remove from the heat and set aside.

◈ In a large saucepan over medium heat, warm the vegetable oil. Add the onions, salt and pepper and sauté until the onions are lightly browned, about 10 minutes. Add the garlic and sauté for 1–2 minutes longer. Add the beans and their liquid and the stock or water. Bring to a boil, reduce the heat to medium and simmer uncovered, stirring occasionally, until the beans start to break apart, 20–30 minutes. Remove the beans from the heat and let cool slightly.

◈ Meanwhile, make the salsa: In a bowl, stir together the tomatoes, onion, cilantro, lime juice and salt and pepper to taste. Cover and refrigerate until you are ready to serve.

◈ Working in batches, transfer the bean mixture to a blender and purée until smooth. Transfer the purée to a clean saucepan and reheat over low heat, stirring frequently, until hot. (If not serving immediately, keep warm over very low heat, stirring often.)

◈ Ladle the soup into warmed shallow bowls and top each serving with a spoonful of salsa and a dollop of *crema* or sour cream.

Serves 6

Tortilla Soup

This hearty soup, a favorite in central Mexico but served throughout the country, results from cooking leftover tortillas with other cantina staples: onion, garlic, chilies and salsa. When left for a few hours, the soup will thicken, and can be thinned with more liquid or served as a starchy side dish.

2 tablespoons vegetable oil
1 yellow onion, diced
1 teaspoon salt
2 cloves garlic, minced
1 dried chipotle chili pepper, stemmed and seeded (optional)
1½ cups (12 fl oz/375 ml) red salsa *(recipe on page 14)*
5 cups (40 fl oz/1.25 l) chicken stock, vegetable stock or water
½ lb (250 g) corn tortilla chips

GARNISHES
¼ cup (⅓ oz/10 g) coarsely chopped fresh cilantro (fresh coriander)
½ small yellow onion, diced
1 lime, cut into 6 wedges

◆ In a saucepan over medium heat, warm the vegetable oil. Add the onion and salt and cook, stirring occasionally, until golden brown, about 15 minutes. Add the garlic and the chipotle chili, if using, and cook for 1–2 minutes longer. Then add the salsa and stock or water and bring to a boil. Reduce the heat to medium-low and simmer, uncovered, for about 20 minutes to blend the flavors. Stir in the tortilla chips and simmer until the chips soften and begin to break apart, 10–15 minutes longer.

◆ Remove and discard the chipotle chili, if used. Ladle the soup into warmed bowls and garnish each serving with cilantro and onion. Squeeze a wedge of lime over each bowl, then drop the wedge into the bowl. Serve immediately.

Serves 6

Pork Stew with Green Chilies

One of the most widespread ways to cook and serve pork in Mexico, and a staple of lunch counters, this hearty dish highlights the rich, slowly cooked meat with the sharpness of tomatillos and the heat of chilies.

1½ lb (750 g) tomatillos, husked

4 lb (2 kg) pork butt or shoulder, trimmed of fat and cut into 2-inch (5-cm) cubes

2 teaspoons salt

1 teaspoon freshly ground black pepper
All-purpose (plain) flour for dusting

¼ cup (2 fl oz/60 ml) vegetable oil

3 yellow onions, cut into 1-inch (2.5-cm) squares

2 fresh Anaheim or poblano chili peppers, stemmed, seeded and cut into 1-inch (2.5-cm) squares

2 fresh jalapeño chili peppers, stemmed, seeded and finely chopped

2 green bell peppers (capsicums), seeded, deribbed and cut into 1-inch (2.5-cm) squares

3 cloves garlic, finely minced

1 tablespoon dried oregano, crumbled

2 teaspoons ground cumin

2 tablespoons coriander seeds, crushed and soaked in water to cover for 15 minutes, then drained

2 bay leaves

¼ cup (⅓ oz/10 g) coarsely chopped fresh cilantro (fresh coriander)

4 cups (32 fl oz/1 l) chicken stock

☒ Preheat a broiler (griller). Place the tomatillos in a shallow pan and place in the broiler about 2 inches (5 cm) from the heat source. Roast, turning occasionally, until charred on all sides, 5–8 minutes. Remove from the broiler and, when cool enough to handle, core and chop the tomatillos. Set aside.

☒ Sprinkle the pork on all sides with the salt and black pepper. Spread some flour on a plate and dust the pork with the flour to coat evenly, tapping off any excess. In a heavy-bottomed frying pan over medium-high heat, warm the vegetable oil. Working in small batches, add the pork cubes and brown well on all sides, 3–5 minutes. Using a slotted spoon, transfer the pork to a large soup pot.

☒ Discard any fat remaining in the frying pan and place the pan over medium heat. Add the onions and sauté, stirring occasionally, until soft, about 5 minutes. Add all of the chilies and bell peppers and sauté until fragrant, 3–4 minutes. Add the garlic and sauté for 1–2 minutes longer.

☒ Transfer the sautéed onions and peppers to the soup pot. Add the chopped tomatillos, oregano, cumin, coriander seeds, bay leaves, cilantro and chicken stock and bring to a boil. Reduce the heat to low and simmer gently, uncovered, until the pork is tender when pierced with a fork, 2–3 hours.

☒ Taste and adjust the seasonings, then spoon the stew into warmed bowls and serve hot.

Serves 6–8

Main Courses

One of the most appealing features of cantina cooking is the scent of savory juices as they drip onto glowing coals and vaporize, transforming into aromatic wisps of smoke that lure customers from blocks away.

Grilled main courses are a hallmark of Mexico's casual cuisine, taking full advantage of the ease with which food may be cooked over an open fire. The keeper of a tiny market stall will build that fire in a small metal drum, while a big taco stand on the plaza keeps its coals ablaze beneath a grill as big as a bed. At home, the recipes on the following pages work just as well on a backyard barbecue, or, if weather or space does not permit, on a stove-top grill or under a broiler.

Of course, other cooking methods are found in cantinas, too, including the gentle simmering used to enhance traditional Mexican moles; the baking essential to enchiladas; and the high-heat frying that forms the golden crust of chiles rellenos. What these dishes have in common with grilled foods is the relative economy and ease with which they are prepared—and the fact that their taste is every bit as delicious as the wonderful aromas that fill the air while they cook.

81

Grilled Beef Tacos

In the beef-eating north, taco stands everywhere feature some form of charcoal-grilled skirt steak. Offer an array of condiments, letting guests fill warm, handmade tortillas to taste. Try the tacos with flour tortillas, too, just as they are often served in northern Mexico.

QUICK SALSA

4	ripe plum (Roma) tomatoes, seeded and coarsely chopped
2	fresh serrano chili peppers, stemmed and coarsely chopped
3	tablespoons fresh lime juice
1	teaspoon salt
½	teaspoon freshly ground black pepper

GARNISHES

¼	cup (⅓ oz/10 g) coarsely chopped fresh cilantro (fresh coriander)
2	avocados, pitted, peeled and diced
2	tomatoes, seeded and diced
6	green (spring) onions, including the tender green tops, sliced on the diagonal
¼	head white cabbage, shredded
1½	lb (750 g) trimmed skirt, flank or tri-tip steaks Salt and freshly ground black pepper
2	cloves garlic, minced
2	tablespoons olive oil Juice of 1 lime
18	small or 12 large corn tortillas, homemade *(recipe on page 13)* or purchased

☒ Prepare a fire in a charcoal grill.

☒ To make the salsa, in a food processor fitted with the metal blade, combine the tomatoes, chilies, lime juice, salt and black pepper and purée until very smooth. Pour into a bowl and set aside. You should have about 1¼ cups (10 fl oz/310 ml). Prepare all the garnishes and place in separate bowls.

☒ Ten minutes before the grill is ready, season the steaks evenly with salt and black pepper, rub with the garlic and olive oil and then drizzle evenly with the lime juice.

☒ Just before grilling the steaks, warm the tortillas on the grill: Fill a shallow pan with water and, one at a time, briefly dip each tortilla in the water and immediately place on the grill rack. Grill for 30 seconds, then turn and grill for 30 seconds longer. Stack the tortillas as they come off the grill and wrap them in a damp towel and then in aluminum foil until serving. (They will keep warm for up to 30 minutes.)

☒ When the fire is very hot, place the steaks on the grill rack about 3 inches (7.5 cm) from the coals and grill, turning once, until evenly caramelized on the outside but still pink in the center, 1–2 minutes per side.

☒ Transfer the steaks to a cutting board and let rest for 3–5 minutes before slicing. Using a sharp knife, cut across the grain into slices ¼ inch (6 mm) thick. Serve immediately with the warmed tortillas, salsa and garnishes. Let diners assemble their own tacos at the table.

Serves 6

82

Chicken Mole Drumsticks

Although the extravagantly spiced, sometimes chocolate-enriched sauces known as moles can be quite complicated, everyone raves about their depth of flavor. This simplified recipe takes only an hour or so to make, but you may still want to cook up a double batch and freeze half. Serve with plenty of white rice.

12	large chicken drumsticks
	Salt
	Freshly ground black pepper
5	dried mulato chili peppers
3	dried pasilla chili peppers
2	dried ancho chili peppers
5	cups (40 fl oz/1.25 l) boiling water
¼	cup (2 fl oz/60 ml) vegetable oil
1	yellow onion, diced
2	cloves garlic, minced
2	tablespoons skinless peanuts
2	tablespoons golden raisins (sultanas)
4	tomatillos, husked, peeled and chopped
1	corn tortilla, homemade *(recipe on page 13)* or purchased, lightly toasted over an open flame and broken into small pieces
¼	teaspoon aniseeds
6	coriander seeds
1	whole clove
10	whole peppercorns
½	cup (1½ oz/45 g) sesame seeds
1½	cups (12 fl oz/375 ml) chicken stock
1	oz (30 g) bittersweet chocolate, coarsely chopped
4	limes, cut into wedges

❖ Rinse the chicken drumsticks and pat dry. Sprinkle with salt and pepper and set aside.

❖ Stem, core, seed and derib all the chilies. In a large, heavy-bottomed pot over medium heat, toast the chilies, turning once, until fragrant and the skins begin to blister, 3–5 minutes. Transfer the chilies to a heatproof bowl, add the boiling water and let stand until cool. Working in batches, transfer the cooled chilies and their soaking water to a blender and purée until smooth. Transfer to a bowl. Set the purée and the blender aside. Wipe the pot clean.

❖ Place the pot over medium heat and add the vegetable oil. When the oil is hot, add the drumsticks and brown well on all sides, about 10 minutes. Using tongs, transfer the drumsticks to a serving dish and keep warm. Add the onion to the same pot and sauté over medium heat until golden, about 10 minutes. Add the garlic and sauté for 1 minute, then add the peanuts and raisins and continue to sauté for 1 minute longer. Stir in the tomatillos and tortilla and cook, stirring occasionally, until soft, about 5 minutes. Remove from the heat and set aside.

❖ In a small, dry frying pan over medium heat, toast the aniseeds and coriander seeds until fragrant, 2–3 minutes. Transfer to a spice grinder or a mortar, add the clove and peppercorns and grind or pulverize until coarsely crushed.

❖ In the same small, dry pan over medium heat, toast the sesame seeds, stirring often, until golden, about 3 minutes. Add half of the seeds to the blender and reserve half for garnish. Add the reserved sautéed vegetables (do not wash the pot), ground spices and chicken stock to the blender. Purée until smooth.

❖ Add the puréed chilies to the same large pot used to sauté the vegetables. Cook over low heat, stirring often in the fat remaining in the pot, until thickened, 8–10 minutes. Add the puréed vegetables and chocolate and season to taste with salt. Stir well. Add the chicken pieces, cover and simmer gently over low heat until the chicken is tender and opaque throughout when pierced with a knife, about 45 minutes.

❖ Serve the drumsticks generously topped with the sauce. Sprinkle with the reserved sesame seeds and garnish with lime wedges.

Serves 6

Grilled Skirt Steak with Onion-Cilantro Relish

Spicy marinades are well suited to hearty cuts of meat like skirt steak. Take care not to marinate the steak too long, though, or the meat will be tough and stringy. The marinade is excellent with pork, lamb or chicken, too. Serve with fresh tortillas and refried beans (recipes on pages 12–14).

CHILI-VINEGAR MARINADE
4   dried Anaheim chili peppers
4   dried árbol chili peppers
2   teaspoons cumin seeds
1   clove garlic, minced
1   fresh jalapeño chili pepper, stemmed, seeded and coarsely chopped
½   cup (4 fl oz/125 ml) red wine vinegar
½   cup (4 fl oz/125 ml) olive oil
1½   teaspoons salt

1   lb (500 g) trimmed skirt steak

ONION-CILANTRO RELISH
1   small white onion, minced
1   fresh serrano chili pepper, stemmed, seeded and minced
½   cup (¾ oz/20 g) coarsely chopped fresh cilantro (fresh coriander)
1   teaspoon salt
    Juice of 1 lime
1   tablespoon olive oil

☙ To make the marinade, remove the stems from all the dried chilies, then shake out and discard the seeds. Place the chilies in a small saucepan with water just to cover. Bring to a boil, remove from the heat and let stand for 20 minutes to soften. Drain.

☙ In a small, dry frying pan over medium heat, toast the cumin seeds until lightly browned and fragrant, 2–3 minutes. In a blender, combine the softened chilies, cumin seeds, garlic, jalapeño chili and red wine vinegar. Purée until thick and smooth, 1–2 minutes. Add the olive oil and salt and blend again until well mixed.

☙ Place the skirt steak in a shallow nonaluminum dish and pour the marinade over it. Let marinate at room temperature for 1 hour.

☙ Prepare a fire in a charcoal grill or preheat a broiler (griller).

☙ Just before placing the steak on the grill or in the broiler, make the relish: In a small bowl, stir together the onion, serrano chili, cilantro, salt, lime juice and olive oil. Set aside until you are ready to serve.

☙ When the fire is hot or the broiler is ready, place the steak on the grill rack about 3 inches (7.5 cm) from the coals, or place in a broiler pan at the same distance from the heat source. Grill or broil, turning once, until seared on the outside but still pink in the center, 1–2 minutes per side.

☙ To serve, slice the steak across the grain and on the diagonal. Arrange the slices on a platter and serve with the relish on the side.

Serves 4

Grilled Citrus-Marinated Chicken Breast

Mexican cooks often marinate chicken in citrus juices before grilling. Don't marinate the meat longer than overnight, however, or it will become too soft. When grilling, sear the skinless side first to seal in the juices, then finish cooking more slowly off to one side of the grill. Serve with green rice (recipe on page 15) and refried black beans (page 14).

1　cup (8 fl oz/250 ml) fresh orange juice

2　tablespoons fresh lime juice

1　dried chipotle chili pepper, stemmed and seeded

1　cup (8 fl oz/250 ml) red salsa *(recipe on page 14)*

¼　cup (2 fl oz/60 ml) olive oil

1　teaspoon salt

4　boneless chicken breast halves
　　Fresh orange slices, optional
　　Fresh cilantro (fresh coriander) sprigs, optional

❧ In a small saucepan, combine the orange juice, lime juice and chili pepper and bring to a boil. Reduce the heat to medium and simmer, uncovered, until the chili is plump, about 5 minutes. Remove from the heat and let cool.

❧ Transfer the cooled citrus mixture to a blender and add the salsa, olive oil and salt. Purée until smooth.

❧ Rinse the chicken breasts and pat dry. Place the chicken breasts in a shallow nonaluminum dish. Pour the purée evenly over the top, cover and let marinate in the refrigerator for 2–4 hours.

❧ Prepare a fire in a charcoal grill or preheat a broiler (griller).

❧ When the fire is hot or the broiler is ready, remove the chicken breasts from the marinade. Place them skin side down on the grill rack about 5 inches (13 cm) from the coals, or arrange them skin side up on a broiler pan and place in the broiler about 4 inches (10 cm) from the heat source. Grill or broil for 2–3 minutes. Turn and cook on the second side for 2–3 minutes. Continue to cook the chicken, turning every 2–3 minutes to avoid burning, until tender and opaque throughout. The total cooking time should be 12–20 minutes, depending upon the size of the breasts.

❧ Transfer the chicken to a warmed platter. Garnish with orange slices and cilantro sprigs, if desired, and serve immediately.

Serves 4

Vegetable Enchiladas

*At its most basic, an enchilada is a tortilla dipped in chili sauce. This unusual variation
pleases even avid meat eaters with a vegetarian filling inspired by rustic potato dishes and enriched
by popular Mexican cheeses. Add rice and beans or a tossed salad for a memorable feast.*

POTATO-AND-PEPPER FILLING

¾   lb (375 g) red potatoes, unpeeled

3   fresh poblano chili peppers, roasted, peeled and seeded *(see glossary, page 125),* then cut into julienne strips

2   red bell peppers (capsicums), roasted, peeled and seeded *(see glossary, page 124),* then cut into julienne strips

½   yellow onion, diced

1   cup (4 oz/125 g) shredded panela or Monterey Jack cheese

½   cup (2 oz/60 g) grated Cotija, Romano or Parmesan cheese

ANCHO SAUCE

1   tomato

4   dried ancho chili peppers, stemmed and seeded

2   cups (16 fl oz/500 ml) hot tap water

1   teaspoon salt

½   teaspoon freshly ground pepper

¼   yellow onion, coarsely chopped

2   cloves garlic, chopped

1   teaspoon ground cumin

1   teaspoon distilled white vinegar

2   teaspoons dried oregano, crumbled

2   tablespoons olive oil

  Vegetable oil for frying

12   corn tortillas, homemade *(recipe on page 13)* or purchased

☙ To make the filling, in a saucepan, combine the potatoes with water to cover. Bring to a boil over medium-high heat. Boil gently until the potatoes are tender when pierced with a fork, about 15 minutes. Drain and let cool, then cut the unpeeled potatoes into ½-inch (12-mm) dice. Place in a bowl. Add the poblano chilies, bell peppers, onion and both cheeses and stir to mix well. Set aside.

☙ To make the sauce, preheat a broiler (griller). Place the tomato in a small shallow baking pan. Place in the broiler 4–6 inches (10–15 cm) from the heat source. Broil (grill), turning occasionally, until charred on all sides, 10–12 minutes. Remove from the broiler, let cool slightly and cut out the core. Set aside.

☙ In a small, dry frying pan over medium heat, toast the chilies, turning once, until fragrant and the skins begin to blister, 3–5 minutes. Remove from the heat and let cool, then place the chilies in a bowl, add the hot water and let soak for 15 minutes to soften.

☙ Transfer the chilies and their soaking liquid to a blender and add the salt, pepper, onion, garlic, cumin, vinegar, oregano and roasted tomato. Purée until smooth, then strain through a sieve into a shallow bowl.

☙ In a heavy-bottomed pot over medium heat, warm the olive oil. Add the purée and cook, stirring constantly, until the sauce thickens slightly, 5–10 minutes.

☙ Meanwhile, preheat an oven to 350°F (180°C). Spread a 12-inch (30-cm) square of plastic wrap on a work surface.

☙ In a shallow frying pan over medium heat, pour in the vegetable oil to a depth of ¼ inch (6 mm). When the oil is hot, fry the tortillas one at a time, turning once, until limp but not crisp, about 30 seconds per side. Using tongs, transfer the tortillas to paper towels to drain. One at a time, dip each limp tortilla in the sauce and then lay it on the plastic wrap. Place about one-twelfth of the filling on the tortilla in a line not quite to the edge of the round and roll up the tortilla. As the tortillas are filled, place them seam side down and side by side in a warmed glass or ceramic baking dish. When all the enchiladas are made, top each one with a few spoonfuls of the remaining sauce.

☙ Place the enchiladas in the oven until warmed throughout, 10–15 minutes. Serve hot.

Serves 4–6

Grilled Shrimp with Mango Salsa

Perfect for a hot summer night, this tropical dish partners grilled seafood with the exotic sweetness of mangoes and the punch of cilantro. Although mangoes are native to India, they came to the New World via Brazil in the 1700s, and are now widely available all over Mexico. The salsa complements fish or chicken as well.

2   cups (16 fl oz/500 ml) olive oil
8   cloves garlic, thinly sliced
    Juice of 2 limes
1   teaspoon salt
½   teaspoon freshly ground black pepper
2   lb (1 kg) large shrimp (prawns), peeled and deveined (20–24 shrimp)

MANGO SALSA
2   ripe mangoes
6   green (spring) onions, including tender green tops, thinly sliced
2   fresh jalapeño chili peppers, stemmed, seeded (if desired) and finely diced
¼   cup (⅓ oz/10 g) coarsely chopped fresh cilantro (fresh coriander)
    Juice of 2 limes
1   teaspoon salt

    Lime wedges, optional

☙ In a frying pan over medium heat, warm the olive oil. Add the garlic and cook, stirring occasionally, until soft, 3–5 minutes. Remove from the heat, pour into a shallow non-aluminum dish and let cool. Add the lime juice, salt and pepper. Mix well.

☙ Using bamboo skewers, thread 4 or 5 shrimp onto each skewer, passing the skewer through points near both the head and tail sections of each shrimp. Place the skewers in the olive oil mixture, turning to coat evenly. Cover and let marinate in the refrigerator for at least 2 hours or up to 12 hours.

☙ To make the salsa, peel each mango and cut the flesh from the pit. Cut into ¼-inch (6-mm) dice and place in a bowl. Add the green onions, chilies, cilantro, lime juice and salt. Stir to mix, cover and refrigerate for at least 30 minutes before serving.

☙ Prepare a fire in a charcoal grill.

☙ When the fire is hot, place the skewers on the grill rack about 3 inches (7.5 cm) from the coals and grill, turning once, until the shrimp turn pink and are opaque throughout, about 3 minutes per side.

☙ To serve, arrange a bed of salsa on each plate and top with a skewer of shrimp, or remove the shrimp from each skewer and arrange atop the salsa. Garnish with lime wedges, if desired, and serve.

Serves 4–6

Fish Fillets in a Bath of Garlic

Garlic sauce, known as mojo de ajo, *is a favorite topping for Mexican seafood. This version adds a touch of ancho chili. Make the sauce quickly while the fish finishes cooking, and take care not to brown the garlic or chilies. Serve with red or white rice (recipes on page 15).*

6   halibut or sea bass fillets, 6 oz (185 g) each
     Salt to taste, plus 1 teaspoon
     Freshly ground black pepper to taste, plus ½ teaspoon
8   tablespoons olive oil
20 cloves garlic, thinly sliced
1   dried ancho chili pepper, stemmed, seeded and chopped
⅔ cup (5 fl oz/150 ml) fish stock or bottled clam juice
     Juice of 3 limes
½ cup (¾ oz/20 g) coarsely chopped fresh flat-leaf (Italian) parsley

✵ Preheat an oven to 350°F (180°C).

✵ Sprinkle the fish fillets with salt and pepper. Place a large cast-iron or other heavy-bottomed frying pan over medium-high heat. When hot, add 3 tablespoons of the olive oil. When the oil is hot, add the fish fillets and sear, turning once, until lightly golden on both sides, 1–2 minutes per side. Transfer the fillets to an ovenproof platter or shallow baking dish and place in the oven to finish cooking until opaque throughout, 3–5 minutes depending upon thickness of fillets.

✵ Meanwhile, add the remaining 5 tablespoons olive oil to the same pan and place over medium-low heat. Add the garlic, the 1 teaspoon salt and the ½ teaspoon black pepper.

Sauté for 1–2 minutes. Add the ancho chili and continue to sauté until fragrant, 1–2 minutes longer. Add the fish stock or clam juice and any juices that have collected in the platter or dish holding the fish fillets and raise the heat to medium-high. Boil until reduced by half, 1–2 minutes. Add the lime juice and parsley and bring to a boil, then remove from the heat.

✵ Pour the sauce over the fish fillets on the platter. Or, if using a baking dish, transfer the fillets to a warmed platter and pour the sauce over the top. Serve immediately.

Serves 6

Grilled Lobster Rosarita

A renowned specialty of seaside cantinas in the Baja California enclave of Rosarita Beach, grilled lobster is served all along the Mexican coast. Maine lobsters and spiny lobsters from tropical waters both work fine. Serve with refried pinto beans, steamed white rice and warm corn tortillas (recipes on pages 13–15).

4	live lobsters, 1½ lb (750 g) each
	Sea salt to taste, plus 1–2 teaspoons
	Freshly ground black pepper to taste, plus 1 teaspoon
3	tablespoons olive oil
6	shallots, chopped
2	cloves garlic, minced
3	fresh red jalapeño chili peppers, stemmed, seeded and chopped
3	fresh green jalapeño chili peppers, stemmed, seeded and chopped
2	teaspoons ground cumin
2	teaspoons paprika
½	teaspoon cayenne pepper
	Juice of 2 limes
2–4	tablespoons unsalted butter
	Lime wedges

☙ Prepare a fire in a charcoal grill or preheat a broiler (griller).

☙ Using a sharp knife, pierce the lobsters between their eyes to kill them. Working with 1 lobster at a time, place back side up and, starting where the tail and head sections meet, cut in half lengthwise, first cutting the tail portion and then the head. Pull out and discard the intestinal vein and any organs. Season the meat to taste with salt and black pepper. Repeat with the remaining lobsters.

☙ Just before you are ready to cook the lobsters, in a wide sauté pan over medium heat, warm the olive oil. When it is hot, add the shallots and sauté until lightly golden, 3–5 minutes. Add the garlic and the jalapeños and continue to sauté for 1–2 minutes longer. Add the cumin, paprika and cayenne pepper and cook, stirring, until the aromas are released but the spices are not burned, 1–2 minutes. Remove from the heat and stir in the lime juice, butter, 1–2 teaspoons salt and 1 teaspoon black pepper.

☙ Place the lobsters on the grill rack shell side down 3–5 inches (7.5–13 cm) from the coals, or arrange them shell side up on a broiler pan and place in the broiler at the same distance from the heat source. Grill or broil, rotating the lobster halves onto their sides and moving them away from the hottest part of the fire as necessary to prevent burning, until the meat is opaque, about 8 minutes. (Do not turn the meat directly toward the fire at any point.)

☙ Spoon the butter mixture over the lobsters during the last few minutes of grilling. Serve hot with plenty of lime wedges.

Serves 4

Chorizo and Roasted Pepper Ragout over Quinoa

Shop around for the finest chorizo available, and take care not to overcook it. Quinoa, an ancient grain native to the South American Andes and prized for both its flavor and nutrients has been rediscovered in recent years. Here, the tiny, round grains make a splendid bed for juicy sausages and a vegetable topping.

QUINOA

3   tablespoons unsalted butter
1   cup (3 oz/90 g) broken vermicelli
½   yellow onion, diced
6   cups (48 fl oz/1.5 l) chicken stock or water
3   cups (14 oz/440 g) quinoa (organic, if possible)

RAGOUT

2   tablespoons olive oil
1   yellow onion, cut into julienne strips
4   cloves garlic, minced
2   teaspoons paprika
1   teaspoon ground cumin
2   red bell peppers (capsicums), roasted, peeled and seeded *(see glossary, page 124),* then cut into julienne strips
2   green bell peppers (capsicums), roasted, peeled and seeded, then cut into julienne strips
2   fresh poblano chili peppers, roasted, peeled and seeded *(see glossary, page 125),* then cut into julienne strips
1   cup (8 fl oz/250 ml) chicken stock
    Salt and freshly ground black pepper
6   large chorizo sausages

❧ Prepare a fire in a charcoal grill or preheat a broiler (griller).

❧ To prepare the quinoa, in a saucepan over medium heat, melt the butter. Add the vermicelli and cook, stirring often, until the noodles turn golden brown, 4–6 minutes. Add the onion and sauté until the onion is soft and begins to turn golden, 3–5 minutes. Add the stock or water and bring to a boil. Add the quinoa and return to a boil. Reduce the heat to medium, cover and cook until the centers of the grains are soft, 20–30 minutes.

❧ Meanwhile, make the ragout: In a large saucepan over medium heat, warm the olive oil. Add the onion and sauté until it begins to turn golden, 3–4 minutes. Add the garlic and continue to sauté for 1–2 minutes longer. Stir in the paprika and cumin and cook for 1 minute. Add all the bell peppers, the chilies and the chicken stock and cook uncovered, stirring occasionally, until the mixture thickens, 10–15 minutes. Season to taste with salt and pepper.

❧ While the peppers are cooking, place the sausages on the grill rack about 3 inches (7.5 cm) above medium-hot coals, or arrange them on a broiler pan and place in the broiler at about the same distance from the heat source. Grill or broil, turning often, until cooked throughout, 8–10 minutes.

❧ To serve, spoon the quinoa onto a warmed platter or individual plates and arrange the sausages on the quinoa. Top with the pepper mixture and serve.

Serves 4–6

Chiles Rellenos

From season to season, region to region and even field to field, poblano chilies can vary in hotness: the only way to test their heat is to taste one. These stuffed chilies can be made and refrigerated up to a day ahead. If the cheese filling is too rich for you, add more vegetables such as corn kernels or peas.

⅓ lb (155 g) Manchego or Monterey Jack cheese, grated

¼ lb (125 g) panela or farmer cheese, grated

2 oz (60 g) añejo or Romano cheese, grated

8 fresh poblano chili peppers, roasted and peeled *(see glossary, page 125)* but kept whole

½ cup (2½ oz/75 g) all-purpose (plain) flour

4 eggs, beaten

½ teaspoon salt

½ teaspoon freshly ground black pepper
Vegetable oil for frying

1 cup (8 fl oz/250 ml) red salsa *(recipe on page 14)*

1 cup (8 fl oz/250 ml) green salsa *(recipe on page 14)*

6 tablespoons (3 fl oz/90 ml) *crema* or sour cream, optional

☒ In a bowl, combine the cheeses and toss to mix. Make a lengthwise slit in each chili and remove the stem, seeds and ribs. Mold ½ cup (2 oz/ 60 g) of the cheese mixture into a torpedo shape and place it inside a chili. Fold the chili around the cheese to enclose it completely and set aside while filling the remaining 7 chilies in the same way.

☒ Preheat an oven to 350°F (180°C). Spread the flour on a plate. In a wide bowl, using a whisk, beat the eggs until foamy, 3–5 minutes. Then whisk in the salt and pepper and set aside.

☒ In a wide cast-iron frying pan over medium heat, pour in the vegetable oil to a depth of 1 inch (2.5 cm) and heat until almost smoking (about 375°F/190°C). Working with 1 chili at a time, dip it in flour and turn to coat, patting off any excess. Dip 2 chilies at a time into the beaten

eggs, then slip them into the hot oil. Fry until lightly browned, 2–4 minutes. Flip and brown the other side, 2–4 minutes longer. Using a slotted spoon, transfer to a paper towel–lined baking sheet to drain. Repeat with the other chilies.

☒ When all the chilies have been browned, remove the paper towel and place the baking sheet in the oven until the cheese at the center of each chili has melted, 4–6 minutes.

☒ To serve, coat one half of each of 4 individual plates with red salsa and the other half with green salsa. Place 2 chilies on each plate and spoon a dollop of *crema* or sour cream on top, if desired. Serve immediately.

Serves 4

Desserts

*C*omida hecha, compañía deshecha, goes an old Mexican saying that censures fair-weather friends: "The meal finished, the company departs." As cantina cooks know from experience, however, there is no better way to hold the attention of a diner than to serve an enticing dessert.

Cantina-style desserts understandably tend toward recipes that can be made ahead of time and keep well, such as moist cakes, rich puddings and iced concoctions. As in the savory courses that come before them, they feature locally grown ingredients, from the citrus fruits of the subtropics to the coconuts and bananas of the tropical regions to the chocolate of the Aztec court. Not surprisingly, good Mexican-grown coffee offers the perfect complement to the naturally assertive flavors.

All of these ingredients, along with those that feature in the other desserts on the following pages, serve another important function, that of soothing the palate after a meal that was more likely than not spiced with chili peppers. Frozen desserts like ice cream or sorbet literally lower the heat, while creamy sweets such as rice pudding or Mexico's national dessert, flan, offer a calming conclusion to such a vibrant repast.

Creamy Lime Pie

The perfect end to a chili-spiced meal, this easy pie cools and soothes the taste buds even as its sharp, citrusy flavor continues to excite them. When choosing limes for the recipe, look for ones that are yellowish and soft when squeezed; they'll provide more juice and more flavor.

1   recipe empanada dough *(recipe on page 34)*, chilled

¾   cup (6 fl oz/180 ml) fresh lime juice

1   lb (500 g) cream cheese, at room temperature

1   can (14 fl oz/440 ml) sweetened condensed milk
    Finely grated zest of 1 lime

1   cup (8 fl oz/250 ml) *crema* or crème fraîche

¼   cup (1 oz/30 g) confectioners' (icing) sugar

1   lime, for garnish

◢ On a lightly floured work surface, roll out the dough into a round about 12 inches (30 cm) in diameter and ¼ inch (6 mm) thick. Drape the round over the rolling pin and transfer to a 9- or 10-inch (23- or 25-cm) glass or ceramic pie plate. Ease the pastry into the pie plate, pressing it gently against the bottom and sides. Trim the edges, leaving a generous ½-inch (12-mm) overhang. Fold the overhang under, then crimp the edges decoratively. Cover and chill for 30–60 minutes.

◢ Preheat an oven to 350°F (180°C). Prick the bottom and sides of the pastry with a fork. Line the pastry with parchment (baking) paper or waxed paper, allowing the edges to hang over the sides and fill with pie weights or dried beans. Bake until only very lightly browned, 20–25 minutes. Remove from the oven and immediately remove the weights and paper. Transfer the pie shell to a rack and let cool completely.

◢ In a food processor fitted with the metal blade, combine the lime juice, cream cheese and condensed milk. Process until smooth, scraping down the sides of the work bowl often. Add the lime zest and process to mix thoroughly. Pour into the pie shell and place in the refrigerator.

◢ In a bowl, using a whisk, beat the *crema* or crème fraîche and confectioners' sugar until soft peaks form. Using a rubber spatula, spread the mixture over the top of the pie, creating peaks evenly over the surface. Slice 8 thin rounds from the center of the lime and cut each round once from the center to the edge. Form a twist from each round and place these twists, evenly spaced, on the pie.

◢ Cover and chill for 4–6 hours or as long as overnight before serving.

Makes one 9- or 10-inch (23- or 25-cm) pie; serves 8

Mexican Wedding Cookies

Different regional variations of light, crumbly cookies like these are served on special occasions—be it weddings, christenings or Christmas—throughout Mexico. The fact that you're just as likely to find such recipes in German cookbooks as in Mexican ones is evidence of the cuisine's rich blending of cultures.

1 lb (500 g) unsalted butter, at room temperature

1 cup (4 oz/125 g) confectioners' (icing) sugar, plus extra for dusting

2 tablespoons vanilla extract (essence)

1 teaspoon salt

2 cups (8 oz/250 g) finely chopped pecans

5 cups (15 oz/470 g) sifted cake (soft-wheat) flour

◐ Preheat an oven to 350°F (180°C). Butter 2 baking sheets.

◐ In a bowl, using an electric mixer set on medium speed, beat together the butter and the 1 cup (4 oz/125 g) confectioners' sugar until light and fluffy, 10–15 minutes. Add the vanilla, salt and pecans and beat just until combined. Using a wooden spoon, stir in the flour, being careful not to overmix.

◐ Form the dough into torpedo shapes about the size of small walnuts and place on the prepared baking sheets. Bake just until very lightly browned on the bottoms, 10–12 minutes, switching pan positions halfway through baking.

◐ Remove from the oven and set the baking sheets on wire racks to cool. Place confectioners' sugar in a large bowl. When the cookies are cool enough to handle, place a few at a time in the bowl and toss gently to coat them on all sides. As the cookies continue to cool, occasionally toss them again with sugar, trying to coat with as much sugar as possible. When fully cooled, serve the cookies or place in an airtight container and store at room temperature for up to 1 week.

Makes about 50 cookies

Vanilla Caramel Flan

*The universal dessert of the Mexican cantina, flan offers a true test of baking skill, so keep
your eye on the oven for the perfect moment to remove the custard. This version is extra caramelly;
be sure to cook the sugar very slowly to coax it to just the right degree of darkness.*

CARAMEL
1½ cups (12 oz/375 g) sugar
1   cup (8 fl oz/250 ml) water

FLAN
2   cups (16 fl oz/500 ml) milk
2   cups (16 fl oz/500 ml) half-
     and-half (half cream)
¾   cup (6 oz/185 g) sugar
8   whole eggs, plus 4 egg yolks
1   tablespoon vanilla extract
     (essence)
     Boiling water, as needed

Preheat an oven to 325°F (165°C).

To make the caramel, in a saucepan over medium heat, combine the sugar and water. Cook, swirling the pan occasionally, until the mixture begins to turn golden, 12–15 minutes. Reduce the heat to low and continue cooking and swirling occasionally until the mixture is dark brown and smells of caramel, about 5 minutes.

Remove the caramel from the heat and pour into a 9-inch (23-cm) round cake pan or eight ¾-cup (6-fl oz/180-ml) custard cups. Using a kitchen towel or hot pad, tilt the pan or cups, swirling the caramel to coat the bottom and sides evenly. Let stand for a few minutes; the caramel will cool down and form a layer about ¼ inch (6 mm) thick on the bottom and sides. Then pour the excess caramel back into the saucepan it was cooked in.

To make the flan, pour the milk into the saucepan holding the excess caramel and place over low heat. Cook, stirring frequently, until the caramel has dissolved in the milk, 3–5 minutes. Strain the warm milk mixture through a fine-mesh sieve set over a bowl. Add the half-and-half and stir to mix well. Add the sugar,

whole eggs and egg yolks, and vanilla. Whisk until blended, then strain through the fine-mesh sieve into the prepared pan or cups. Set the pan or cups in a roasting pan and place the roasting pan in the oven. Pour boiling water into the roasting pan to reach halfway up the sides of the cake pan or custard cups.

Bake until the center of the custard(s) feel just firm when pressed gently with the fingertips, 45–55 minutes for the large pan or 30–40 minutes for the individual cups. Remove from the oven and let cool for about 1½ hours. Then cover with plastic wrap and refrigerate overnight or for up to 4 days.

To serve, run a knife along the inside edge of the pan or cups to loosen. Invert a serving dish over the pan or a saucer over each cup. Quickly invert and carefully lift off the pan or cup. Carefully pour excess caramel into a small sauce pitcher.

Serve chilled. Offer the extra caramel alongside.

Serves 8

Spiced Apple Cake with Guava Cream Cheese

This fragrant spice cake, laden with fresh apples, goes together quickly. If you can't find guava jam in your area, feel free to substitute plum, cherry or any other preserves you have on hand. The cake is also terrific at brunch, where it pairs well with a cup of great coffee.

APPLE CAKE
2   eggs
1   cup (8 fl oz/250 ml) vegetable oil
¼   cup (2 fl oz/60 ml) fresh orange juice
2   cups (1 lb/500 g) sugar
2   cups (10 oz/315 g) all-purpose (plain) flour
4   teaspoons ground cinnamon
1   teaspoon salt
2   teaspoons baking soda (bicarbonate of soda)
4   cups (1 lb/500 g) peeled, cored and finely chopped Granny Smith or other tart green apples (about 4 apples)
1   cup (4 oz/125 g) walnuts, coarsely chopped

GUAVA CREAM CHEESE
¼   cup (3 oz/90 g) guava jam
1   tablespoon fresh lime juice
⅔   cup (5 oz/155 g) cream cheese, at room temperature

☒ Preheat an oven to 325°F (165°C). Butter and flour a 10-inch (25-cm) round cake pan.

☒ To make the cake, in a bowl and using an electric mixer set on medium speed, beat the eggs until frothy, 3–4 minutes. Add the vegetable oil and orange juice and mix thoroughly. In a separate bowl, stir together the sugar, flour, cinnamon, salt and baking soda. Add the flour mixture to the egg mixture and beat on low speed until thoroughly combined. Fold in the apples and walnuts.

☒ Pour the batter into the prepared pan. Bake until firm to the touch and a toothpick inserted into the center comes out clean, about 1 hour; cover the top with aluminum foil if it begins to overbrown. Remove from the oven and let cool in the pan on a rack for 5 minutes, then invert onto the rack. Let cool completely.

☒ Meanwhile, make the guava cream cheese: In a bowl, combine the jam, lime juice and cream cheese. Using a fork, mash and stir briskly until light and fluffy.

☒ To serve, place the cake on a serving plate. Using an icing spatula or knife, spread the guava cream cheese evenly over the top.

Makes one 10-inch (25-cm) cake; serves 8

Tangerine Sorbet in Chocolate Shells

After a feast, when you think you couldn't eat even one more bite, this superb sorbet makes a perfect dessert. Fruit ices are popular in Mexico, and this version heralds the abundant tangerine season. The lacy chocolate cups dress up the dessert for a special dinner party.

TANGERINE SORBET

2	tablespoons grated tangerine zest
3½	cups (28 fl oz/875 ml) fresh tangerine juice (18–20 tangerines)
½	cup (4 fl oz/125 ml) fresh lemon juice (3 or 4 lemons)
1¼	cups (10 oz/315 g) sugar
¼	cup (2½ fl oz/75 ml) light corn syrup

CHOCOLATE SHELLS

½	cup (2 oz/60 g) ground blanched almonds
½	cup (2½ oz/75 g) all-purpose (plain) flour
¼	cup (2½ fl oz/75 ml) light corn syrup
¼	cup (2 oz/60 g) sugar
¼	cup (2 oz/60 g) unsalted butter
1	oz (30 g) unsweetened chocolate
½	teaspoon vanilla extract (essence)

Shredded tangerine zest for garnish, optional

☒ To make the sorbet, in a bowl, combine the tangerine zest and juice, lemon juice, sugar and corn syrup. Stir until the sugar dissolves. Transfer to an ice cream maker and freeze according to the manufacturer's instructions. Pack into a freezer container and place in the freezer until set, 2–4 hours.

☒ Preheat an oven to 350°F (180°C). Butter a baking sheet.

☒ To make the chocolate shells, in a bowl, stir together the almonds and flour until thoroughly mixed. In a small, heavy-bottomed saucepan over low heat, combine the corn syrup, sugar, butter and chocolate. Heat, stirring constantly, until the mixture just comes to a boil. Remove from the heat and stir in the vanilla. Add the flour mixture and stir until fully blended.

☒ Drop the dough by tablespoonfuls onto the prepared baking sheet, leaving at least 3 inches (7.5 cm) on all sides to allow room for spreading and forming no more than 4 shells on the sheet. Bake until they spread out and are lacy, 8–10 minutes. Remove from the oven and let cool for 1–1½ minutes. Using a thin metal spatula, lift the baked rounds from the baking sheet and drape each round over an inverted coffee cup. Let cool completely, then carefully lift off the shells and set aside. Repeat with the remaining dough, to form 8 shells in all. (The shells can be stored in an airtight container for up to 3 days.)

☒ To serve, place the shells on small dessert plates. Fill each shell with an equal amount of the sorbet and garnish with tangerine zest, if desired. Serve immediately.

Serves 8

Date Ice Cream with Almond Crunch Topping

Ultrasweet dates, a favorite Mexican sweet, always seem to prompt a craving for ice-cold milk, so it makes perfect sense to feature them in this milky concoction. The crunchy topping will keep for weeks in an airtight container in the refrigerator, ready for any sundae you make.

ALMOND CRUNCH TOPPING

½   cup (1½ oz/45 g) old-fashioned rolled oats

½   cup (2½ oz/75 g) hulled pumpkin seeds

½   cup (2½ oz/75 g) chopped almonds

1½ tablespoons vegetable oil

1½ tablespoons honey

1½ tablespoons apple juice

⅛   teaspoon salt

DATE ICE CREAM

2   cups (16 fl oz/500 ml) nonfat milk

1   lb (500 g) fresh dates, preferably medjool

6   egg yolks

¾   cup (6 oz/185 g) firmly packed brown sugar

3   cups (24 fl oz/750 ml) half-and-half (half cream)

2   teaspoons vanilla extract (essence)

☙ To make the crunch topping, preheat an oven to 300°F (150°C). Lightly oil a baking sheet or line it with parchment (baking) paper.

☙ In a bowl, combine the oats, pumpkin seeds and almonds and stir to mix. In a small saucepan over low heat, combine the vegetable oil, honey, apple juice and salt and stir until combined, the salt has dissolved and the mixture is warm. Pour the warm honey mixture over the oat mixture and toss to coat evenly. Spread out the mixture on the prepared baking sheet and bake, stirring occasionally, until golden, about 20 minutes. Transfer to a rack and let cool, then pack in a small airtight container and place in a freezer until needed.

☙ To make the ice cream, pour the milk into a saucepan and place over low heat. Heat, stirring often with a wooden spoon, until only 1 cup (8 fl oz/250 ml) remains, about 20 minutes. Remove from the heat and let cool completely.

☙ Remove the pits from the dates and chop into pea-sized pieces. Place half of the pieces on a plate and place in the freezer until needed. Place the remaining date pieces in a blender, add the cooled milk and purée until smooth.

☙ In a bowl, combine the egg yolks and brown sugar and whisk vigorously until lemon colored. In a saucepan, bring the half-and-half to a rolling boil and immediately pour over the yolk mixture while whisking constantly. Add the date-milk mixture and the vanilla, mix well and set aside to cool completely.

☙ Transfer to an ice cream maker and freeze according to the manufacturer's instructions. Stir the reserved date pieces into the ice cream and pack into a freezer container. Place in the freezer until set, 2–4 hours.

☙ To serve, scoop into chilled ice cream dishes, top with the almond crunch topping and serve at once.

Makes 1½ qt (1.5 l); serves 6

Banana Coconut Cake

Sweet bananas are grown predominantly along the Gulf Coast, where they are frequently cooked with butter and sugar and then flambéed. This extra-moist cake combines them with coconut, a favorite ingredient in Mexican candies. Look for wide shards of flaked coconut in health food stores.

CAKE

¾ cup (6 oz/185 g) plus 2 table-spoons unsalted butter, at room temperature

1½ cups (12 oz/375 g) sugar

3 eggs

½ cup (4 fl oz/125 ml) buttermilk

1⅓ cups (11 oz/345 g) mashed ripe banana

2½ cups (7½ oz/235 g) sifted cake (soft-wheat) flour

1 teaspoon baking powder

¾ teaspoon salt

¾ teaspoon baking soda (bicarbonate of soda)

½ cup (2 oz/60 g) finely chopped pecans

COCONUT CUSTARD

¾ cup (6 fl oz/180 ml) plus 1 tablespoon unsweetened coconut milk

1 cup (8 fl oz/250 ml) whole milk

½ cup (4 oz/125 g) sugar

¼ cup (1 oz/30 g) cornstarch (cornflour)

4 egg yolks

TO ASSEMBLE CAKE

3 bananas, peeled and sliced

¼ cup (2 fl oz/60 ml) lemon juice

2 tablespoons sugar

1 cup (4 oz/125 g) unsweetened flaked or shredded dried coconut, toasted *(see glossary, page 125)*

☙ Preheat an oven to 350°F (180°C). Butter and flour two 9-inch (23-cm) round cake pans. To make the cake, in a large bowl and using an electric mixer set on medium speed, beat together the butter and sugar until light and fluffy, about 10 minutes. Beat in the eggs, one at a time. Continue beating until very light and fluffy, about 10 minutes longer. Mix in the buttermilk and mashed banana.

☙ In a separate bowl, sift together the flour, baking powder, salt and baking soda. Add the flour mixture to the butter mixture and beat on low speed just until moistened. Increase the speed to medium and beat for 1 minute. Then, using a wooden spoon, fold in the pecans.

☙ Pour the batter into the prepared pans, dividing it evenly. Bake until a toothpick inserted into the center comes out clean, 25–35 minutes. Transfer to racks and let cool in pans for 5 minutes, then invert the cakes onto the racks to cool completely.

☙ Meanwhile, make the custard: Line a rimmed baking sheet with parchment (baking) paper or plastic wrap and set aside. In a heavy sauce-pan, combine the coconut milk and whole milk and bring to a boil. Remove from the heat and set aside.

In a bowl, stir together the sugar and cornstarch. Add the eggs yolks and stir briskly until blended. Whisk half of the hot milk into the sugar-yolk mixture to temper it, then whisk the sugar-yolk mixture into the remaining hot milk in the saucepan. Place over medium heat and cook, stirring constantly, until smooth and thick, 3–4 minutes. Spread the custard on the prepared baking sheet; cover with a sheet of parchment paper or plastic wrap to prevent a skin from forming. Refrigerate until cool.

☙ Preheat an oven to 350°F (180°C).

☙ To assemble the cake, in a bowl, toss the banana slices with the lemon juice and sugar. Trim the top of a cake layer so that it is level and place on a serving plate. Spread with a thin layer of the custard, arrange the banana slices on top, and then spread a thin layer of custard over the bananas. Place the second cake layer on top, bottom down, and spread the top with the remaining custard. Garnish with the coconut, mounding it on top. Serve at once or cover and refrigerate for up to 24 hours.

Makes one 9-inch (23-cm) cake; serves 8

Kahlúa Chocolate Bread Pudding

*Everybody in Mexico loves chocolate, which is often partnered with the taste of cinnamon
and coffee. Here, those three flavors combine in a bread pudding that, although rustic in origin,
makes an elegant presentation when served warm with a drizzle of sauce and cream.*

PECAN STREUSEL
1   cup (4 oz/125 g) pecans
¼   cup (2 oz/60 g) firmly packed
       brown sugar
¼   cup (1½ oz/45 g) all-purpose
       (plain) flour
1   teaspoon ground cinnamon
¼   teaspoon salt
3   tablespoons chilled unsalted butter

PUDDING
4   oz (125 g) unsweetened chocolate
¾   cup (6 oz/185 g) firmly packed
       brown sugar
1½   cups (12 fl oz/375 ml) heavy
       (double) cream

CUSTARD
6   whole eggs, plus 2 egg yolks
¾   cup (6 oz/185 g) granulated
       sugar
1   teaspoon vanilla extract (essence)
¾   loaf day-old French bread, about
       ¾ lb (375 g), cut into ½-inch
       (12-mm) cubes

KAHLÚA SAUCE
6   tablespoons (3 oz/90 g) unsalted
       butter
1   cup (8 fl oz/250 ml) Kahlúa or
       other coffee liqueur
½   cup (4 oz/125 g) granulated
       sugar
1   egg

Unsweetened whipped cream

☙ To make the streusel, preheat an oven to 325°F (165°C). Spread the pecans on a baking sheet and toast until lightly browned and fragrant, about 10 minutes. Remove from the oven, let cool and chop coarsely. Leave the oven set at 325°F (165°C). In a bowl, combine the nuts, brown sugar, flour, cinnamon, salt and butter. Using your fingertips, mix until crumbly. Set aside in a cool place.

☙ To make the pudding, butter an 8½-by-4½-inch (21.5-by-11.5-cm) glass loaf pan and dust with granulated sugar. Place the chocolate in a heatproof bowl and set over (not touching) simmering water in a pan. Heat, stirring constantly, until the chocolate melts. Add the brown sugar and cream and whisk until smooth. Remove from the heat and set aside.

☙ To make the custard, in a large bowl, combine the whole eggs and egg yolks, sugar and vanilla. Whisk until well mixed. Add about ½ cup (4 fl oz/125 ml) of the custard to the chocolate mixture to temper it, whisking vigorously. Then add the chocolate mixture to the remaining custard and whisk until blended. Add the bread cubes, stir to coat evenly and let stand until the bread has absorbed the liquid, about 15 minutes.

☙ Pour the pudding-custard mixture into the prepared loaf pan. Top evenly with the pecan streusel and set in a roasting pan. Place in the oven and add boiling water to reach halfway up the sides of the loaf pan. Bake until the center feels slightly firm to the touch, about 2 hours.

☙ While the pudding is baking, make the Kahlúa sauce: Place the butter in a heatproof bowl over (not touching) simmering water in a pan. When the butter has melted, add the Kahlúa and sugar and whisk until the sugar has dissolved. Whisk in the egg and cook over simmering water until slightly thickened, about 10 minutes. Strain through a fine-mesh sieve into a serving pitcher.

☙ Remove the pudding from the oven and let cool slightly. Cut into 6–8 equal pieces and place on dessert plates. Pour a pool of the Kahlúa sauce along one side of each piece of pudding and place a spoonful of whipped cream on the other side. Serve at once.

Serves 6–8

Rum Raisin Rice Pudding

Rice pudding runs a close second to flan (recipe on page 108) as Mexico's favorite dessert. While some special-occasion versions might add a splash of brandy to the recipe, this variation nods to the Caribbean by including raisins that have been plumped in rum.

1 cup (7 oz/220 g) short-grain white rice
4 cups (32 fl oz/1 l) nonfat milk
4 cinnamon sticks
1 can (14 fl oz/440 ml) sweetened condensed milk
1 vanilla bean, split lengthwise
Ice water, as needed
¾ cup (6 fl oz/180 ml) dark rum
1 cup (6 oz/185 g) golden raisins (sultanas)
Ground cinnamon

❧ Rinse the rice in several changes of water until the water runs clear. Drain well.

❧ In a saucepan, combine the nonfat milk and cinnamon sticks and bring to a boil over medium-high heat. Add the rice and return to a boil. Reduce the heat to medium-low and cook uncovered, stirring occasionally, until the centers of the grains are just barely soft, 12–15 minutes.

❧ Add the sweetened condensed milk to the rice mixture and then scrape the seeds from the vanilla bean halves into the pan. Add the vanilla pods as well, stir to combine, cover and continue to simmer over low heat until the rice is plump and tender and the sauce is the consistency of heavy (double) cream, 10–15 minutes longer. Remove from the heat and place over a bowl of ice water to stop

the cooking. Stir the mixture occasionally as it cools. When cool, discard the vanilla pods and cinnamon sticks, transfer to a bowl, cover and refrigerate until well chilled, about 2 hours.

❧ Meanwhile, in a heavy-bottomed saucepan over low heat, combine the rum and raisins. Simmer until the raisins have plumped and the rum is almost gone, about 5 minutes. Remove from the heat and let cool.

❧ Fold the raisins into the chilled rice pudding. Serve icy cold with a dusting of ground cinnamon on top.

Serves 4–6

Chocolate Nut Tart

Really a pecan pie with a Mexican twist, this luscious tart is perfect for holiday entertaining.
Although elegant, it is also heartwarmingly homey, which explains why you might also see something
like it on the countertop of a Mexico City cafetería, ready to be served to the lunchtime crowd.

PASTRY DOUGH
½ cup (4 oz/125 g) unsalted butter,
   at room temperature
1⅓ cups (5½ oz/170 g) confectioners'
   (icing) sugar
1 egg
1 teaspoon salt
1¾ cups (9 oz/280 g) all-purpose
   (plain) flour

CHOCOLATE-NUT FILLING
3 eggs
¾ cup (5½ oz/170 g) firmly
   packed brown sugar
½ cup (5 fl oz/155 ml) dark corn
   syrup
2 tablespoons dark molasses
6 tablespoons (3 oz/90 g) unsalted
   butter, melted
2 teaspoons vanilla extract (essence)
2 teaspoons ground cinnamon
1 teaspoon salt
2 cups (9 oz/280 g) slivered
   blanched almonds
¾ cup (4 oz/125 g) chopped
   semisweet chocolate

Unsweetened whipped cream

☒ To make the pastry dough, in a bowl, combine the butter and confectioners' sugar. Using a wooden spoon, cream together until very light and fluffy. Add the egg and salt and beat until combined. Add the flour and stir until the mixture comes together to form a dough. Divide the dough in half and pat each half into a ball. Wrap in plastic wrap and refrigerate 1 ball for 2–3 hours or as long as overnight. Reserve the other half to make another tart; it can be frozen for up to 2 months.

☒ Preheat an oven to 325°F (165°C).

☒ On a lightly floured work surface, roll out the ball of dough into a round about 12 inches (30 cm) in diameter and ⅛–¼ inch (3–6 mm) thick. Drape the round over the rolling pin and transfer to a 10-inch (25-cm) tart pan with a removable bottom. Ease the pastry into the tart pan, pressing it gently against the bottom and sides. Trim the edges even with the pan rim. Place in the refrigerator to chill for 15 minutes.

☒ Prick the bottom and sides of the pastry with a fork. Bake until golden, 10–12 minutes. Transfer to a rack to cool. Leave the oven set at 325°F (165°C).

☒ To make the filling, in a large bowl, whisk together the eggs, brown sugar, corn syrup, molasses, melted butter, vanilla and cinnamon until well blended. Add the salt, almonds and chocolate and mix to coat evenly.

☒ Pour the filling into the tart shell and bake until the center is set, 35–40 minutes. To test, press gently on top with your fingertips. Transfer to a rack and let cool.

☒ To serve, remove the pan sides and, using a spatula, slide off the pan bottom onto a serving plate. Cut into wedges and serve with whipped cream.

Makes one 10-inch (25-cm) tart;
serves 6–8

Glossary

The following glossary defines common ingredients and cooking techniques, as well as cooking equipment, used in Mexican kitchens.

Avocado

Native to Mexico, the avocado tree bears a pear-shaped fruit with leathery skin that conceals buttery, pale green flesh. While several varieties of avocado are commonly available, varying in size, color and texture of skin, the finest flavor and consistency belong to Hass avocados, which are small to moderate in size and have dark, rough skin.

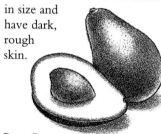

Bay Leaves

The dried leaves of the bay laurel tree give their pungent, spicy flavor to simmered dishes.

Beans

Beans are a staple of the Mexican kitchen. Before use, dried beans should be carefully picked over to remove small stones or fibers or any discolored or misshapen beans. Many need also be soaked in cold water for several hours to rehydrate them and thus shorten their cooking time.

Some popular varieties used in this book include:

Black Small beans with black skins, smoky flavor and a mealy texture. Sometimes called turtle beans, black beans (2) are common along the Gulf Coast and in southeastern Mexico.

Kidney These kidney-shaped beans (1) have reddish brown skins, a robust flavor and a slightly mealy texture.

Pinto This brown-and-tan speckled variety (4)—its name means "painted"—has a rich flavor and mealy texture.

Red Widely available small beans (3) with brownish red skins and a slightly sweet flavor.

Bell Peppers

Sweet, bell-shaped red, yellow or green peppers, also known as capsicums, are popular in cantina dishes.

Bell peppers must have their indigestible seeds removed before use. Often the peppers are also roasted, which loosens their skins for peeling and enhances their natural sweetness.

TO SEED A BELL PEPPER

Cut the pepper in half lengthwise and cut or pull out its stem and seeds, along with the white ribs, or veins, to which the seeds are attached.

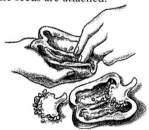

TO ROAST AND PEEL A BELL PEPPER

Seed the pepper as directed and place the halves, cut sides down, on a baking sheet. Place under a preheated broiler (griller) until the skins blister and turn a deep brown. Remove from the broiler and place the peppers in a plastic or paper bag. Seal and let steam for 10 minutes. Remove from the bag and peel off the skins.

Chayote

This pear-shaped member of the squash family has a mild flavor and moist texture reminiscent of cucumbers or zucchini (courgettes). Although one variety has dark green, prickly skin, most chayotes available outside Mexico have relatively smooth, pale green skin.

Cheeses

While most Mexican cheeses may be found outside of the country only in ethnic markets, several kinds of more commonly available non-Mexican cheeses serve well as substitutes.

Añejo "Aged" white cheese with a dry, crumbly texture and salty flavor. Grated Romano, Parmesan or feta may be substituted.

Asadero Literally a "roasting" cheese, this mild, soft white variety is typically used for melting. Mozzarella or Monterey Jack may be substituted.

Cabrales Spanish goat's milk cheese similar in taste to Roquefort. If unavailable, substitute any blue cheese.

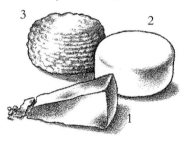

Cotija (1) A type of *añejo* cheese.

Manchego The Mexican variety of this classic Spanish cheese (2) is made from cow's milk and has a fine melting consistency, similar to that of Monterey Jack. Depending on how it is used, other cheeses such as Romano, Parmesan, white Cheddar or Monterey Jack may be substituted.

Panela Fresh cheese (3) with a soft, slightly spongy texture. Depending upon the recipe, Monterey Jack, water-packed fresh mozzarella, dry cottage cheese, farmer cheese or dry ricotta may be substituted.

Chilies

Mexico is the world's largest producer of chilies, with scores if not hundreds of varieties available in the marketplace. Most of a chili's heat resides in its seeds and the white ribs to which the seeds are attached. For milder flavor, remove both before using. Some of the most common varieties, used in this book, include:

Anaheim Fresh, mild to moderately hot green chilies (1), about 6 inches (15 cm) long and 2–2½ inches (5–6 cm) wide. Also called California or long green chilies, and closely related to the New Mexican chili.

Ancho Literally the "wide" chili, this is the dried form of the poblano chili, and measures up to 5 inches (13 cm) long and 3 inches (7.5 cm) wide. Wrinkled and deep reddish brown, it varies in hotness from mild to moderate, and has a slightly bittersweet taste and aroma reminiscent of prunes.

Árbol This widely available, dried, bright red fresh chili, literally a "tree" chili, is very hot. The slender chilies measure about 2½ inches (6 cm) long.

Cayenne Commonly used in its ground dried form, this very hot chili lends subtle heat.

Chipotle Smoked form of the jalapeño, light brown in color, usually packed in a thick sauce called *adobo* or pickled in brine, but also sometimes found simply dried.

Habanero Measuring about 2 inches (5 cm) in length and up to 1¾ inches (4.5 cm) wide, this fresh or dried chili—literally, the Havana chili—is one of the hottest available, more than 30 times hotter than the fiery jalapeño. Besides heat, its flavor is notable for hints of tropical fruit.

Jalapeño Named for the capital of the Veracruz state, this fresh, fairly small (2–3 inches/ 5–7.5 cm long and up to 1½ inches/4 cm in diameter), thick-walled, fiery variety (3) is usually sold green, although red ripened specimens may sometimes be found.

Mulato Similar to the *ancho,* this dried chili tends to have a darker color and a fuller, slightly bitter taste.

Pasilla Up to 6 inches (15 cm) long, narrow and notably wrinkled, this dried chili has a rich, spicy flavor with hints of fruit. Also known as the *chile negro.*

Poblano Moderately mild, fresh green—or sometimes ripened red—chili (2). Large and broad in shape—up to 5 inches (13 cm) long and 3 inches (7.5 cm) wide—it is most commonly stuffed for chiles rellenos or cut into strips as a garnish.

Serrano Widely available, small, slender fresh green or red chili (4)—up to 2 inches (5 cm) long and about ½ inch (12 mm) wide—is about as spicy as the *jalapeño,* although its flavor is notably sharper. Its name translates as "mountain" chili.

TO ROAST AND PEEL
FRESH CHILIES
Roasting fresh chilies develops their flavor, gives them a softer texture and enables their thin, indigestible skins to be peeled off. To roast a chili, hold it with tongs or a fork over a gas stove burner set to a medium flame and turn it until its skin is evenly blackened and blistered, 5–10 minutes. Or cook on a dry *comal* or heavy skillet over medium heat, turning occasionally, until evenly blackened, 10–15 minutes. Cover with a damp cloth or seal in a heavy plastic or paper bag for 10–15 minutes. Then hold under a thin stream of cold running water and peel off the skin.

Chorizo
A spicy Mexican fresh pork sausage, traditionally seasoned with chilies and garlic. Although the ground meat is often sold wrapped in plastic to be shaped into patties and fried, it is also available as fresh whole sausages; look for the whole sausages in well-stocked butcher shops. If unavailable, substitute fresh Cajun andouille or Polish kielbasa.

Cilantro
An indispensable ingredient in Mexican cooking, this fresh, green herb—also known outside of Mexico as fresh coriander or Chinese parsley—has a pungent, bright flavor.

Clam Juice
A convenient substitute for fish stock in seafood dishes, this briny, strained liquid from shucked clams may be found in bottles in most food stores.

Coconut
The fruit of the tropical coconut palm. Coconut milk—a rich extract made by puréeing the fruit's flesh with hot water—is available both in Latin American and Asian markets; do not confuse it with sweetened coconut cream. Unsweetened flakes of dried coconut are sold both in tiny shreds and in wide shards.

To toast coconut, spread on a baking sheet and toast in a 350°F (180°C) oven until lightly golden, about 5 minutes.

Corn Husks
The traditional wrapper for tamales, these dried leaves of the corn plant are commonly sold in plastic bags, sometimes already trimmed and flattened. Store them in a dry place, where they will keep for up to a year. Before use, the brittle leaves must be soaked to make them pliable.

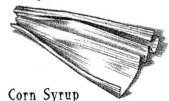

Corn Syrup
Neutral-tasting syrup extracted from corn. Available either as unfiltered dark corn syrup or filtered light corn syrup.

Crema
Used as an enrichment and garnish for both sweet and savory dishes, this Mexican-style cultured cream resembles the crème fraîche of France.

Crème Fraîche
This lightly soured and thickened fresh cream is a French

specialty now sold in many well-stocked markets. To make a similar product at home, lightly whip ½ cup (4 fl oz/ 125 ml) heavy (double) cream; stir in 1 teaspoon sour cream. Then cover and let stand at room temperature until thickened, about 12 hours.

Eggplant, Japanese
Variety of eggplant distinguished by its long, slender shape, fine flesh and relative absence of seeds. Also known as aubergine or Asian eggplant.

Epazote
This Mexican herb has an unfavorable aroma when fresh, but cooked, it lends a pungent dimension of flavor. It is also known as wormseed, Mexican tea and stinkweed. There is no acceptable substitute.

Fennel
This bulb vegetable of Mediterranean origin is prized for its mild anise taste and a crisp, refreshing texture. A related variety of the plant produces feathery leaves used as an herb and small crescent-shaped seeds used as a spice.

Garlic
Although Spaniards introduced garlic to Mexico less than five centuries ago, this aromatic bulb has become an inextricable part of the cuisine. Peel cloves of their thin, papery skin before using.

Jicama
This brown-skinned tropical root looks like a large turnip. Its white flesh, however, resembles a radish in texture and a water chestnut in taste.

Lard
A clarified cooking fat rendered from pork, lard adds a signature richness to many Mexican dishes. The best-quality lard is sold in specialty butcher shops, although packaged varieties are available in some food stores.

Mango
This oval-shaped tropical fruit has sweet yellow-orange flesh, and yellow skin tinged with orange when ripe. A ripe mango will yield slightly to fingertip pressure.

Masa Harina
A fine flour ground from corn kernels that have been soaked in slaked lime, *masa harina*—literally, "dough flour"—is used to prepare the doughs for corn tortillas and tamales. Prepared masa dough—used for making tortillas and tamales—is available in the refrigerator section of Mexican markets.

Milk, Sweetened Condensed
Made by evaporating 60 percent of the water from whole milk, then sweetening it with sugar, this canned product is a popular ingredient in desserts.

Mint
Spearmint and other mints complement the spicy seasonings of Mexican food with their cool sweetness.

Mussels
These bluish black bivalves open to reveal succulent orange-colored flesh. Before cooking, scrub the shells well under running water and pull away the fibrous threads (below)—known as "beards"—by which they attach themselves to rocks and piers. Discard any mussels whose shells are not closed.

Oils
Oils used in this book include:

Olive Oil Extra-virgin olive oil, extracted from olives on the first pressing without use of heat or chemicals, is valued for its distinctive fruity flavor. Products labeled pure olive oil are less aromatic and flavorful and may be used for general cooking purposes.

Peanut Oil An all-purpose cooking oil that possesses a hint of the nut's richness.

Vegetable Oil The name applies to many kinds of all-purpose flavorless oils pressed from vegetables or seeds, including corn oil or safflower oil.

Onions
Like garlic, onions were introduced to Mexico by the Spaniards and have become an indispensable part of the cuisine. The most commonly used types include *green onions,*

also known as spring onions and scallions, a variety harvested immature, with both its small white bulb and its long dark-green leaves enjoyed raw or cooked; *red (Spanish) onions,* a mild, sweet variety with purplish red skin and red-tinged white flesh; *white onions,* a white-skinned, white-fleshed variety that has a sweet, mild flavor and is the most commonly used onion in Mexican kitchens; and *yellow onions,* the familiar white-fleshed, stronger-flavored variety with dry, yellowish brown skins.

Oranges, Blood
A variety of orange with orange skin blushed with red and deep red flesh that has a stronger flavor than regular oranges, which may be substituted.

Oregano
Small-leaved herb noted for its aromatic spicy flavor, which intensifies with drying. Also known as wild marjoram.

Papaya
Prized for their sweet, exotic-tasting flesh, many different sizes, shapes and colors of this tropical fruit are grown in Mexico. Remove the seeds before using. Also known as pawpaw.

Parsley
Of the two varieties of this herb available, flat-leaf parsley, also known as Italian parsley, is preferable, having a more pronounced flavor than the more common curly-leaf type.

Quinoa
This ancient grain, available in health food stores, is rich in nutrients, and has an earthy, pleasantly sour taste.

Shortening, Vegetable
In baked goods, this solid vegetable fat may be used in place of or along with butter or lard, to "shorten" the flour—that is, to make it flaky and tender.

Shrimp
Fished in Pacific and Gulf waters, shrimp (prawns)—both the medium-sized variety commonly sold raw in seafood stores and the smaller, plump rock shrimp—have long been enjoyed in Mexico.

Sour Cream
This commercial dairy product, made from pasteurized cream, is often used as a topping for Mexican dishes.

Spices
Many spices are found in the Mexican kitchen. Those used in this book include:

Cinnamon This popular spice comes from the aromatic bark of a type of evergreen. It is sold as whole dried strips about 3 inches (7.5 cm) in length—cinnamon sticks—or ground.

Coriander These small, spicy-sweet seeds, used whole or ground, come from the green coriander or cilantro plant.

Cumin Although it originated in the Middle East, this dusky, aromatic spice now flavors many Mexican dishes. It is sold either as whole, small crescent-shaped seeds or ground.

Paprika Available in sweet, mild and hot versions, this powdered red spice is derived from dried paprika peppers.

Saffron This golden-orange, exotically perfumed spice is the dried stigmas of a species of crocus. Sold either as whole threads or powdered.

Squash, Summer
In addition to the familiar zucchini (courgette), small, edible-skinned summer squashes include the mild, slightly sweet *yellow crookneck,* which has a bulbous flower end and a slender, curving stem end; the green or golden *straightneck;* and the round, flattened *patty-pan,* distinguished by its scalloped edge and pale green color.

Tomatillos
Also called *tomates verdes,* and sometimes mistakenly referred to as green tomatoes, small green tomatillos are actually related to the Cape gooseberry and have a distinctive sharp, fruity flavor. Fresh tomatillos are usually sold still encased in their brown papery husks.

Peel off the easily removed husks by hand before the tomatillos are cut. Canned tomatillos may be found in most well-stocked markets.

Tomatoes
This vegetable-fruit originated in Peru, traveling northward to southern Mexico before Columbus's voyage to the New World. For the best flavor, use sun-ripened tomatoes in season, whether large red tomatoes, plum (Roma) tomatoes or small red or yellow cherry tomatoes. Out of season, plum tomatoes—whether fresh or canned—offer the best flavor.

Tortilla Press
Made of cast iron or heavy-duty aluminum, this device consists of two flat, circular plates connected by a hinge with a handle that presses them together. A ball of corn *masa,* placed between the two plates and compressed, is formed into a flat, round tortilla.

Vanilla
The dried aromatic pod of a variety of orchid, the vanilla bean is a popular flavoring in Mexican desserts. Although its most common form is that of an alcohol-based extract (essence), the pod and the tiny seeds within it also impart vanilla flavor.

ACKNOWLEDGEMENTS

Mary Sue Milliken and Susan Feniger wish to thank the tireless and creative kitchen staff at their restaurant, Border Grill in Santa Monica, California, with special appreciation to Kajsa Dilger, Doris Chavez, Carlos Mulia and Scott Linquist.

The photographer and stylist would like to thank Cyclamen Studio in Berkeley, California, Caryn and Jon Schulberg, and Patty Hill for lending props for photography.

For their valuable editorial support, the publishers would like to thank: Desne Border for proofreading, Ken Della-Penta for indexing, Regina Cordova for recipe title translations and Tina Schmitz for administrative support.

Index